Monatshefte Occasional Volume Number 2

From Kafka and Dada to Brecht and Beyond

Five Essays by Peter Demetz, Reinhold Grimm,
Egon Schwarz, Walter H. Sokel, and A. Leslie Willson

Edited by

Reinhold Grimm
Peter Spycher
Richard A. Zipser

Published for *Monatshefte*
The University of Wisconsin Press

Sponsored by Oberlin College

Published 1982

The University of Wisconsin Press
114 N. Murray St., Madison, Wisconsin 53715

The University of Wisconsin Press, Ltd.
1 Gower St., London WC1E 6HA, England

First printing

Printed in the United States of America

For LC CIP information see page 87

ISBN 0-299-97014-0

Contents

Foreword

The Max Kade German Lecture Series, a program of lectures by prominent scholars in the field of German literature and culture studies, was established at Oberlin College during the 1975–1976 academic year. From the outset, the purpose of this lecture series has been to bring students, faculty, and other members of the college community together—in both formal and informal settings—with some of the leading Germanists of our day. The Kade lectures are given in English, in order to reach as wide an audience as possible, and they treat topics of general rather than narrow interest. Also, the lecturers are invited to participate in class sessions and seminars, if their talks or areas of specialty happen to coincide with courses being taught at Oberlin.

Listed below, in order of their visits to Oberlin College, are the first five Kade Lecturers and the titles of their talks:

1976-77: A. Leslie Willson
University of Texas at Austin
"The Humanistic Stance of GDR
Author Günter Kunert"

1977-78: Walter H. Sokel
University of Virginia
"Kafka's Poetics of the Inner Self"

1978-79: Peter Demetz
Yale University
"The Challenge of Phonetic Poetry:
On Dada, its Historical Antecedents
and its Developments Today"

1979-80: Reinhold Grimm
University of Wisconsin at Madison
"Confessions of a Poet: Poetry
and Politics in Bertolt Brecht's Lyric"

1980-81: Egon Schwarz
Washington University
"What is Austrian Literature?
The Example of H.C. Artmann
and Helmut Qualtinger"

For the purpose of publication, these lectures have been revised slightly and, wherever necessary, brought up to date. All quotations are now given in German. A few of the original titles have been altered, but the essence of the original content has not. Also, the editors have rearranged the sequence of the lectures; they now appear chronologically in terms of historical development, not in terms of presentation at Oberlin. Since each Kade Lecturer was free to choose his topic, within the loose guidelines alluded to above, their talks are not linked by a single theme—and it is only by coincidence that all of the speakers decided to focus on the 20th century.

In "Kafka's Poetics of the Inner Self," Walter H. Sokel points out that Franz Kafka's " goal was 'truth,' *i.e.*, the perfect *adaequatio* between word and feeling, between linguistic sign and inner being." Kafka was aware of a twofold "truth": a "communal, collective, and universalist" one and a "deeply personal, individual, and subjective" one. These two "truths" represented a conflict for him; but the second mattered more to him, and it is this one that Sokel examines. "The inner self conquers the word by 'filling it out.' It stands in a position of dominance to language. It is to take possession of language and, through language, of the social collective world to which language belongs. . . . Kafka equates the call of literature with a hidden, powerful inner world which . . . stands in complete opposition to ordinary life." It is an artistically mental outpouring that is somewhat comparable to a sexual act. But above all it is a magically messianic one which would "raise the world into the pure, the true, and the unchangeable." The flesh becomes word, as it were. A good work, Kafka believed, can only be written in a single sitting, "unconsciously, without any deliberation and artifice." And the narrative point of view should be a single consciousness, not that of an omniscient narrator. Hence Kafka's difficulties with larger forms of fiction, hence his difficulties with the distractions of human relationships. After *Das Urteil* Kafka thought he recognized duplicity rather than truth in his own writing. "In the ideal of writing, as Kafka conceived it," says Sokel, "the author should be nothing but the medium for what wants to be expressed; but self-reflection steps between the inspiration and the act, and dams up and pollutes the flow from within." And self-reflection may lead to self-absorption, even to narcissism.

In "Varieties of Phonetic Poetry: An Introduction," Peter Demetz states that in modern poetry "sound more often than not prevails over meaning," and this compels us to reflect anew on "the uneasy relationship of sound, meaning, and writing" *(phonopoeia, logopoeia, and graphopoeia)*. There is, of course, nothing wrong with a preponderance of phonopoeia (or, for that matter, of graphopoeia) although, in poetry, logopoeia cannot totally be discarded. After briefly discussing Edgar Allan Poe's sound-imitating poem "The Bell" and noting that this poem "still accepts a traditional consensus about the collaboration of elements," Demetz examines a number of phonetic poems written by different authors between 1916 and 1921. In Hugo Ball's "Katzen und Pfauen," we perceive "sound clearly organized in two systems in which we are urged to hear what irritated cats and peacocks are telling each other." The sounds and sound patterns, strange as they are, are unmistakably related to the German language. Hugo Blümner's "Ango Laina," a supposedly "absolute" sound poem, also depends on German language patterns, even though it is a "dialectical inversion" of German, strenuously trying to avoid common German sounds and sound patterns. As for the poem "Wand" by Kurt Schwitters, it belongs to his *konsequente Dichtung* in which he probes what he terms "internal rhythm." The text "operates with proportions and symmetries which can be formalized in a numerical way." What is deliberately excluded from the text is meaning (but the single word used in it, *Wand*, does seem to have a "semantic direction"). Raoul Hausmann, a radical individualist and creator of verbal "soundings," was interested only in "the way in which the sounds were produced by the human apparatus of articulation," and he regarded his articulatory motor exercises as energy-activating and mystically therapeutical. We readers of poetry would perhaps do well to pay more attention to its "sensual" aspects than just to its "substantive" ones.

In "Confessions of a Poet: Poetry and Politics in Brecht's Lyric," Reinhold Grimm deals with Bertolt Brecht's keenly felt problem of writing "pure" poetry in times of social and political upheaval. Brecht believed that in bad times "pure" poetry (*e.g.*, descriptions of the beauty of nature, or sensuous pleasure, *etc.*) should be replaced by political-social poetry, that art, for the sake of morality, should function as "a weapon." Nevertheless, not only are his political poems aesthetically wrought themselves, but many of them contain "pure" art as well, either explicitly or, in some instances, implicitly, though not without a gesture of denial and a twinge of troubled conscience on the author's part. Brecht, as Grimm puts it, "has a whole series of poems in which the denial of the lyrical is itself elevated to the purest lyrical expression"; he "makes use of the 'evocation through negation,' which banishes the naturally beautiful and humanly round into the realm of nothingness and thereby summons them into existence and permanence."

In A. Leslie Willson's " 'Grenzverschiebung': Günter Kunert's Humanistic Stance," Kunert, GDR writer in West German exile, is shown as an avowed communist but, above all, a true humanist who has stressed values ignored or suppressed by the GDR authorities: *e.g.*, man's individuality; social equity for all (including women and Jews); the transitoriness, fragility, and imperfection of human existence, as well as our memory of the past; the importance of communication without censorship. Writing is, for Kunert, discovering, self-understanding, self-liberation, self-realization; it is a *Grenzverschiebung*, an extension of limits. Reading is a process of sublimation. Kunert's pessimism and irony, genuinely human stances, were not appreciated by the GDR regime. Now living in the North of West Germany, no longer in his beloved Berlin, he once again "admonishes and cautions and remains pessimistic, but he also retains his deep belief in the essential good and right of human beings. His utterances are made in the unmistakable voice of humanity."

In "What Is Austrian Literature? The Example of H.C. Artmann and Helmut Qualtinger," Egon Schwarz reminds us that the idea of a given literature has customarily been based on the idea of a given national character or spirit, an allegedly timeless quality or essence. Such ideas have much to do with nationalism and conservatism (and, in extreme cases, with fascism). "During Austria's post-World War II period of restoration," these misconceptions lingered on, even well into the 1960's. It must be recalled, however, that, as Schwarz says, "the Danubian monarchy was much too fragmented into ethnic, linguistic, and geographic subdivisions, held together by mainly dynastic interests, to have produced a single unified literature." The First Republic lacked identity and a sense of direction. The Second Republic "is more homogeneous . . ., surer of itself, and more prosperous. It is possible that in the course of time it will create conditions for an Austrian literature truly representative of its culture." The fact is that the definition of a national literature, and specifically that of an Austrian literature, can only be sought through a historically oriented approach. For "a work of literature is Austrian if it demonstrably issues from Austrian social history or can convincingly be shown to have a bearing on it." Thus, a scholar studying the Austrianness of Austrian literature should consult historians, particularly social and psycho-historians, and should constantly bear in mind historical continuities as well as discontinuities (*e.g.*, those of language and of what Schwarz calls tradition). "The vertical rise of the Viennese dialect . . . into higher levels of society since World War II is [a] dynamic change and probably accounts for phenomena like Artmann and Qualtinger." H.C. Artmann, in his *med ana schwoazzn dintn*, removed Viennese dialect from its closeness to "the people"; Helmut Qualtinger, on the other hand, cabaretist and social critic, has confronted Viennese and Austrian conditions in a direct way, especially through his creation of "Herr Karl," a member of the lower middle class, an Austrian version of *Vergangenheitsbewältigung*, but with universal dimensions. Schwarz arrives at the conclusion that "despite [Artmann's and Qualtinger's] opposing stances as a *l'art pour l'art* and an *engagé* writer respectively, they have more in common than meets the eye trained only in textual analysis or blinded by preconceived notions. This common ground is provided by the Viennese social milieu." However, with regard to Austrian literature, Schwarz cautions that "one will have to focus on relatively small units of time, space, and society to determine the mode of interaction between literary works and the epochs in which they originated."

The annual Kade lectures have been made possible through a number of generous grants to the German section of Oberlin College's German and

Russian Department by the Max Kade Foundation (New York City). Like the Max Kade German Writer-in-Residence program, which has become a tradition at Oberlin and gained an international reputation, the Kade Lecture Series is an event that all of us in the humanities look forward to. Whereas the German-speaking writers have enriched our lives each year through their presence on campus and their imaginative works, the Kade Lecturers have engaged us through the lively presentation and discussion of their ideas.

We at Oberlin College, a community of teachers and students, artists and scholars, have profited immensely from the generosity of the Max Kade Foundation over the years. It now seems only fitting that the lectures presented to us, by five of the most distinguished Germanists in the United States, should be collected and shared with others at home and abroad.

Peter Spycher / Richard A. Zipser

Kafka's Poetics of the Inner Self

Walter H. Sokel

When Kafka began to write, scepticism toward the writer's medium—language—and despair over the limitations inherent in it, were widespread, and not only in German and Austrian letters, although with special acuteness in these. The earliest piece of writing by Kafka which is preserved, an entry in a young girl's album, dating from the year 1900, is a striking document of this *Sprachkrise* or *Sprachskepsis*, the crisis of faith in language.[1] Kafka, age seventeen, declares his impatience with the inadequacy of words for the task of conveying the intimate and inward aspect of memory, an inwardness which the German word for memory, "Erinnerung," etymologically suggests: "Als ob Worte erinnern könnten! Denn Worte sind schlechte Bergsteiger und schlechte Bergmänner. Sie holen nicht die Schätze von den Bergeshöhn und nicht die von den Bergestiefen" (B 9).[2]

Kafka's earliest letters to his friend Oskar Pollak are marked by a profound disillusionment with the possibilities of genuine communication through language. The nature of language as a tool of generalizing and conceptual communication endangers the task of expressing essentially personal and intimate truths. Kafka's analogy of words to "bad mountaineers" and "bad miners" of the soul closely resembles another document of the *Sprachkrise,* Maurice Maeterlinck's passage from *Le Trésor des humbles,* which Robert Musil chose as the motto for his novel *Törleß*, composed three years after Kafka's album entry:

> Sobald wir etwas aussprechen, entwerten wir es seltsam. Wir glauben in die Tiefe der Abgründe hinabgetaucht zu sein, und wenn wir wieder an die Oberfläche kommen, gleicht der Wassertropfen an unseren bleichen Fingerspitzen nicht mehr dem Meere, dem er entstammt. Wir wähnen eine Schatzgrube wunderbarer Schätze entdeckt zu haben, und wenn wir wieder ans Tageslicht kommen, haben wir nur falsche Steine und Glasscherben mitgebracht; und trotzdem schimmert der Schatz im Finstern unverändert.[3]

Here we find the same critical questioning of language, the same denunciation of its inadequacy as in Kafka's earliest extant written statement. Language, in the process of utterance, devaluates and falsifies its content. It cannot do justice to, and fails to retain, the essence of what we wish to say. In the most famous document of the *Sprachkrise*, Hugo von Hofmannsthal's "Ein Brief," Lord Chandos says that if we could "think with the heart" expression would present no problem;[4] but such a language of the heart is given to us, if at all, only in rare moments of mystical enchantment. To some extent, this "critique of language," to use the title of Fritz Mauthner's three-volume work of 1903, reveals discontent with the worn-out, cliché-ridden, and pretentious idiom of much of late 19th-century writing—a discontent of which Karl Kraus became the outstanding exponent. However, the critique of language also envisages an inherent incapacity of words, insofar as words derive their being from generalizing thought, to express a highly individualized sensibility and inwardness. The social-utilitarian realm which language serves is held to bear no relationship to that inwardness of the individual which Hofmannsthal calls "the heart," and which Maeterlinck and Kafka designate by analogies to the depths of the sea or the interior of the earth. If we were to compare the linguistic concerns of these writers to the problems of communication encountered by Kierkegaard's Abraham in *Fear and Trembling*, the close relationship of the *Sprachkrise* to proto-existential thought would become apparent. The *Sprachkrise* possibly contributed more heavily to the Central European reception of Kierkegaard in the first two decades of this century than might be suspected.

However, even more directly relevant to an understanding of the *Sprachkrise*, and particularly to the role it plays in shaping Kafka's poetics, is an approach that benefits from the intellectual categories of Jacques Derrida. For the *Sprachkrise* provides an excellent example of that "metaphysical nostalgia" which, according to Derrida, finds it difficult to accept "l'impossibilité pour un signe . . . de se produire dans la plénitude d'un présent et d'une présence absolue," the impossibility of that "parole pleine qui doit être la vérité."[5] What Derrida diagnoses as metaphysical nostalgia is the desire to abolish "la brisure," the gap between the signifier and "the reality" which is posited behind and beyond the verbal sign. The assumptions underlying the phenomenon of the *Sprachkrise*, and particularly the poetics of Kafka, are understandable in terms of that "ineluctable nostalgia for presence that makes of this heterogeneity [of word and being] a unity by declaring that a sign brings forth the presence of the signified."[6] The *Sprachkrise* is a symptom of the loss of faith in the actuality of such a statement. Its preoccupation would best be described by changing the indicative, "a sign brings forth," into the hortatory subjunctive, "a sign should bring forth the presence of the signified."

In the period between the beginnings of his diary and the writing of *Das Urteil*, Kafka evolved a rudimentary theory of writing which, in its most confident form, seems to embody the intellectual tradition that Derrida associates with metaphysical nostalgia for the "absolute presence" in writing of that reality to which writing refers, a presence which, in Derrida's words, "claims to be truth." Kafka's goal was "truth," *i.e.* the perfect *adaequatio* between word and feeling, between linguistic sign and inner being.[7] This "truth," to be sure, had two aspects pointing in opposite directions. One of those was communal, collective, and universalist, the other deeply personal, individual, and subjective. It is this second aspect of Kafka's "truth" which I want to explore here in some detail. His ideal was "to fill each word entirely with [himself]" (T 34).[8] He strove for the ability to write a tale that he could draw to his breast (T 39). He graphically described how the length of a word written by him would equal exactly the extent of his "feeling" (T 60). He spoke of "dwelling" in each of his thoughts (T 57). He wished to "pour himself" into his writing (T 230). He exulted in the "miracle" that every thought, "even the weirdest," could find words able to express it (T 293). The precise agreement between inner experience and linguistic formulation was his criterion for literary value (T 186f.), and he insisted that where "the right feeling vanishes, writing loses all value" (T 39f.).

This "poetics" presupposes two distinct entities—the inner self or inner world, which is to be expressed, and the medium of expression—language. If perfect correspondence between the two is achieved, writing becomes the true vehicle of being. The fundamental precondition for this harmony does not lie in language, but in the inner world. Being is prior to words. The inner self conquers the word by "filling it out." It stands in a position of dominance to language. It is to take possession of language and, through language, of the social collective world to which language belongs.

In his earliest statement about the nature of his writing, a letter to his friend Oskar Pollak, the twenty-year-old Kafka describes his intention as a writer. It is "to lift, with one single heave, that which I believe I have in me (I do not always believe it)" (B 17). This kind of writing he called "magic." Ten years later, in a diary entry of 1913, he writes of "the enormous world which I have in my head" (T 306) and considers it his special mission and destiny "to liberate [himself] and to liberate it," even at the cost of his life: "Die ungeheure Welt, die ich im Kopfe habe. Aber wie mich befreien und sie befreien, ohne zu zerreißen. Und tausendmal lieber zerreißen, als sie in mir zurückhalten oder begraben. Dazu bin ich ja hier, das ist mir ganz klar" (T 306).

One year after that, he speaks of his special talent of representing his "dreamlike inner life" (T 420) to which all his other potentialities have had to be sacrificed. His diaries show abundantly that his "dreamlike inner life" consisted not only of the most vivid and powerful night dreams, which he frequently wrote down, but also of hallucinatory visions that obsessed him, especially shortly before falling asleep or immediately after waking up, and which greatly contributed to the insomnia of which he bitterly complained all his life. A tumult of deeply troubling oneiric images obsessed, tormented, and exhilarated him. He called these visionary hosts his "devils," "ghosts," and "demons."[9] One example may stand here for many: "Heute mittag vor dem Einschlafen . . . lag auf mir der Oberarm einer Frau aus Wachs. Ihr

Gesicht war über dem meinen zurückgebogen, ihr linker Unterarm drückte meine Brust" (T 162).

These visions, as noted in his diaries, sometimes formed the point of departure for narratives. In a diary entry of late May, 1914, for instance, Kafka begins a fragmentary narrative which tells of a white horse suddenly appearing in an avenue of a city (T 375). Two pages later, while criticizing the fragment, he makes clear how the inspiration for the story had come to him. The white horse had appeared to him the night before in a vision, as he was about to fall asleep. It seemed to have literally stepped out of his head: "Gestern erschien mir das weiße Pferd zum erstenmal vor dem Einschlafen, ich habe den Eindruck als wäre es zuerst aus meinem der Wand zugedrehten Kopf getreten, wäre über mich hinweg und vom Bett hinuntergesprungen und hätte sich dann verloren" (T 377).

This close connection between hallucinatory vision and narrative beginning sheds an interesting light on Kafka's creative method or process in general, even as the specific image of the white horse sheds light on such tales as "Ein Landarzt," in which magic horses play a crucial role, or "Der neue Advokat," in which the protagonist is a horse metamorphosed into a lawyer.

When Dr. Rudolf Steiner, founder of the Anthroposophic branch of the Theosophic movement, visited Prague, Kafka mentioned his visionary states to him. In his writing, he confessed to Dr. Steiner, he had had experiences "close to the clairvoyant states, as described by you, Herr Doktor" (T 57). Kafka's statement receives its full meaning if we recall that Rudolf Steiner had described elaborate methods for attaining extrasensory perceptions and transcendental insights. Perhaps Kafka's visionary states, some of which are described with frightening vividness in his diaries, were similar to hallucinations induced by drugs. In any case, these states seemed to give him feelings of transcending the quotidian self and reaching the frontiers of human potentialities. He found in these states, as he told Dr. Steiner, the "enthusiasm that probably characterizes the clairvoyant," except his peace, and "even that," he adds, was "not entirely" lacking (T 57).

Thus Kafka equates the call of literature with a hidden, powerful inner world which, as the early letter to Oskar Pollak already clearly shows, stands in complete opposition to ordinary life. Physical health and strength, social intercourse, conversations, particularly with women—these are all seen by him as "the alternative" to "the magic" with which writing beckoned. He compares the conjuring up of the buried treasures of the inner self to "a mole's existence"—anticipating by twenty years the key image of his last fragment, "Der Bau"—and concludes his letter with the question whether an active physical and social life might perhaps not have been the real "magic" of his summer. If so, he implies, he would have been wrong to look for it in "the mole and his kind." The conflicting demands of inner and social self dominated Kafka's entire life and work.[10] His letters to Felice Bauer definitively show that he tended to view his existence in terms of a struggle between these two selves.[11]

The struggle between the "two selves" can also be seen in terms of two kinds of linguistic intent—expression and communication, or, in Kafka's case, literature and conversation. In his early letter to Oskar Pollak, Kafka viewed his newly found ability *to talk* (to women), in other words, the social art of conversation, an alternative to the inner-directed "magic" of his writing. We thus encounter the paradox that one form of linguistic utterance, writing, stands in radical opposition to the essential function of language as the privileged form of human communication. This paradox has of course been a familiar one since Romanticism, or at least since Mallarmé's distinction between the "parole immédiate" of ordinary, informative discourse, and the "parole essentielle" of purely evocative poetry.[12] In fact, it is already contained in Kant's concept of "aesthetic ideas." An "aesthetic idea" for Kant is one that no language can ever "completely attain and make comprehensible."[13] Insofar as the "aesthetic idea" is transrational, Kafka's visionary utterances, which withhold any aid to the understanding, might be said to conform to "aesthetic ideas" in the Kantian sense. The visionary statement offers no explanatory context. It cannot "make itself comprehensible." Kafka himself considered his art irrational when he insisted that *The Judgment*, a visionary work of which he was particularly fond, was utterly inexplicable. This, to be sure, did not prevent him from putting his astute analytic intelligence to work at interpreting the tale.[14]

The problem of communicating the "aesthetic idea" lay of course at the core of the phenomenon of *Sprachkrise*. For Kafka this problem became a particularly acute conflict between the demands of the visionary inner world, insisting on being expressed, and the equally strong moral duty to communicate with the human species. As we have seen, Kafka from the beginning viewed the task of communication as the alternative to the "magic" of writing. The relationship between them, and therewith the strategy of Kafka's writing, will become clearer if we examine the contrast between the poetics of the early diaries and the entirely different poetics outlined in Kafka's famous letter to his father, the only sustained attempt at an autobiography which he left us.

Kafka's letter to his father begins by calling attention to his difficulty in communicating. The fear which his father had always instilled in him, Kafka claims, had deprived him of the confidence and power necessary for oral communication. By the terror which he struck in his son, his father had condemned him to be a stutterer. In any conversation he found himself at a loss for words. Max Brod contradicts Kafka's self-portrait in this respect. He presents his friend as a very articulate, sociable, and witty companion. However, if we are to believe Kafka's own statements about himself, Brod's image of him must have been Kafka's skillfully maintained social façade. For in his life documents he, like Jean-Jacques Rousseau, constantly laments his inability to talk coherently and successfully. The archetype of all oral communication remained, for Kafka, communication within his family and, above all, with his father. In this he had miserably failed, in his own view.

Writing, on the other hand, was at the opposite pole. It was the region to which the son could flee and which he cultivated because it was the one area in the world where his father's powerful influence did not extend. Speech was linked to the father's forbidding and threatening presence, but writing dealt with his absence: "Mein Schreiben handelte von Dir, ich klagte dort ja nur, was ich an Deiner Brust nicht klagen konnte" (H 203).[15]

Thus writing memorialized a twofold absence for Kafka—first, the absence of a loving, trusted parent, which had caused his grief initially, and then, the absence of the longed-for audience for this grief. In his writing, Kafka, according to his "Letter," was always bitterly aware of the unbridgeable "difference" between the subject matter and the act of writing. The unreachable father functioned like that "trace" which recalls to us the eternal absence of that which writing is about, and spells out the inevitable heterogeneity which makes writing different from being and gives it its autonomy. What is un-Derridan in the poetics of the "Letter" is the writer's nostalgia for the presence that is withheld. Writing for Kafka is not the confident assertion and affirmation of the "difference," but the everlasting regret of an imposed autonomy.

What Kafka omits from his autobiography is the substitution which his early diaries triumphantly proclaim. The place of the absent father, as the source of inspiration, was taken by the "inner self." Kafka's poetics, at least up to the composition of *The Judgment*, was the attempt to find the way to transcend the need for oral communication which, he felt, his father had made impossible for him. As viewed from Kafka's poetics in the diaries, writing is not the lament over an absence, but the celebration of a presence. This presence, to be sure, is no longer the father, but the inner self and its visionary truth. Kafka's writing, so conceived, represents a victory over the father, and more than that—a victory of the self over the social world of which his father was the earliest representative.

Kafka saw writing, in its ideal form, as a passionate penetration, a taking possession of language, and through language of the social world, originally embodied in the family, that language represents and contains. Kafka's early diaries are filled with recordings of creative experiences in which self-transcendence unites with the sensation of omnipotence. It is this merging of selflessness with self-exaltation which suggests a parallelism between writing and sexuality in Kafka's poetics. Kafka frequently associates inspirational writing with images of flowing, streaming, opening out. He mentions his "pouring himself" into his work, and compares his "outpouring" in his writing to an erotic relationship with a girl of his acquaintance (T 76). Recalling the experience of writing *The Judgment* in the trance-like state of a single night, Kafka writes of an ecstatic self-abandonment, a flowing away of all boundaries of the self, an "absolute opening of body and soul." "Nur so kann geschrieben werden" (T 294), he proclaims apodictically.[16] While writing *The Judgment*, as Max Brod relates, Kafka had experienced an ejaculation.[17] This complete abolishment of the boundaries and limits of the ego, to which the interview with Dr. Steiner also alludes, connects self-transcendence with self-aggrandizement. The loosening of the self seems to bestow magic powers on it: "Das Bewußtsein meiner dichterischen Fähigkeiten ist am Abend und am Morgen unüberblickbar. Ich fühle mich gelockert bis auf den Boden meines Wesens und kann aus mir heben, was ich nur will" (T 76).

In such moments, Kafka felt. any random sentence written down by him would be perfect (T 42). It is, once again, this merging of selflessness with self-exaltation which suggests the sexual aspect of Kafka's poetics. In the early stages of his courtship of Felice Bauer, Kafka made this parallelism between writing and eros explicit. He then saw in his writing the justification for his hope of winning her. Both writing and eros are, in the framework of Kafka's life as presented in his letter to his father, triumphs over the parentally induced inhibition of communication.

However, the essential precondition for successful writing, in Kafka's sense, was the genuineness of "the presence" of the truth in the act of writing. The act would have to be the direct outflow, the "unmediated vision," of the inner self. The "draft" or current of inspiration must never be interrupted. If it were, the truth would be gone, and with it, all the value the work might have. The greatest peril for this writing was self-deception—the writer's delusion that he was still in touch with the truth while it had left him. Kafka's inhibiting perfectionism derives from his insistence upon the presence of the original feeling that inspired the writing. Any work in excess of that feeling, any embellishment or "fill-in," would make the work not only aesthetically worthless, but morally, and one might say ontologically, wrong. This insistence goes beyond the romantic and existentialist cult of authenticity.[18] The anxiety it engenders can be compared to the worshipper's dread of defilement of the Eucharist.

The consequence of this insistence upon the unadulterated presence of the inner truth in the work is Kafka's conviction that a good work can only be written in a single sitting, unconsciously, without any deliberation and artifice. *The Judgment*, he felt, qualified for such standards, and it was the only work of his which he accorded unmixed and even enthusiastic approval. Having written it in one single night, without interruption, so that his legs were stiff when he rose in the morning, he could exclaim: "Nur *so* kann geschrieben werden, nur in solchem Zusammenhang, mit solcher vollständigen Öffnung des Leibes und der Seele" (T 294). From this height of a coherent unity—a "Zusammenhang"—achieved between inspiration and result, he could only look down upon the novel—the first version of *Amerika*—with which he had been struggling for a long time, as on "lowlands" where he had wasted his efforts.

Kafka's contemptuous dismissal of the novel and complete satisfaction with the short tale point to his essential difficulty when faced with narratives that could not possibly be written in one sitting. Inherent in Kafka's approach to writing, it explains the numerous false starts and alternate versions of beginnings of narratives that were never continued beyond a few sentences or paragraphs. Most of his long stories and all his novels remained fragments; and even *Der Prozeß*, Kafka's only novel with an ending, remained fragmentary in the middle and exhibits a mosaic-like structure of episodic scenes. This poetics, which was of course not an arbitrary and controllable choice, but the way in which Kafka's literary imagination seemed to work, also helps to explain the peculiarly painful conflict Kafka experienced between the demands of literature and human life. All human relationships represented fatal distractions from a work that brooked no interruption. Nothing short of the life-long self-confinement in the innermost chamber of a deserted cellar, of which he speaks to Felice, would seem to satisfy such rigorous requirements for concentration.

This explains the paradox that an activity conceived of by Kafka as a flowing outward, an inundation of the world by the inner self, seemed at the same time to require an absolute withdrawal, an inhuman solitude. One of Kafka's earliest diary entries states that "loneliness is best" for him. It "metamorphoses" him—Gregor Samsa's fate is here seen as a most positive occurrence—and has "a power over [him] which never fails" (T 34). For it opens up his "inner self" and allows its deeper layers to come forth. With a dread bordering on panic, he seeks to ward off any disturbance of his creative loneliness. In a letter to Felice, several years later, he describes the ideal way of life for him. It would be to live "with writing utensils and a lamp, in the innermost chamber of a locked spacious cellar." Someone would come to bring him his food, but place it rather far away from his room, "behind the outermost door of the cellar." This arrangement would protect him from contact with the person feeding him. He would return to his desk in the innermost hiding place, and, after eating, "immediately commence to write again! And the things I would then be able to write! From what depths I would tear them out! Without effort! For utmost concentration knows no effort!" (BF 250). To be sure, he adds, at the slightest slackening of inspiration he would probably go mad. He tells her of "invisible chains" binding him "to an invisible literature" and warns her that he would scream "if anyone should come near to touch my chains" (BF 450). That such auspices would not be favorable for his engagement to Felice was not difficult to see.

In his first attempt at a novel, "Hochzeitsvorbereitungen auf dem Lande," Kafka presented the paradigm for the contradictory structure underlying his poetics. The protagonist, Raban, having to visit his fiancée in the country, wishes he could evade this dreary task by repeating in actual life what he had been accustomed to do in a recurrent fantasy of his childhood years. Faced with disagreeable social obligations, Raban imagined that he would separate his real self from his body. The former would stay in bed, in "the shape of a great beetle" (H 12), while his body would be sent to carry out Raban's tasks in the world outside. Meanwhile, Raban's true self, reclining in inhuman and solitary serenity, would be the absolute master, not only of his human façade, but of the entire world. The traffic below Raban's window would be utterly dependent on his whims. By withdrawing from humanity and totally identifying with his true desire, by becoming his truth, Raban is able to dominate the world from which he has withdrawn. This wish dream describes the structure underlying Kafka's inspirational poetics. In Stanley Corngold's formulation, the "omnipotent bug . . . suggests the inwardness of the act of writing."[19] By reducing his empirical person to the zero degree, and uniting with his "dreamlike inner life," the writer by the same token takes possession of society, through its medium—language. His total concentration on his writing immerses him in the essence of his community, as embodied in its language, and enables him to appropriate it so absolutely that he becomes the power that moves it.*

That Kafka pursued messianic ambitions in his writing has often been observed. The passage is frequently quoted in which he writes that he would receive permanent satisfaction from his writing only if he could "raise the world into the pure, the true, and the unchangeable" (T 534). Messianism is the logical consequence of his need "to liberate" "the enormous world in [his] head" into articulated existence. For this inner world would or should be the power that by confronting the empirical world would help it to achieve transfiguration. This messianic task requires the writer to be a Messiah figure. Indeed the state of union between inner self and word that Kafka invokes in his poetics alludes to the incarnation, but reverses its terms. Here it is not the Word become flesh, but the flesh—the living individual of flesh and blood—become Word. "Ich bin nichts als Literatur," Kafka declares. In place of an incarnation we could speak of an "inlogozation." The self achieves divine power through "pouring itself" into the waiting body of language. Kafka, whose writing took place mainly during the night, copies a passage from Roskoff's *History of the Devil* which states that, among the Caribs, "he who works in the night is believed to be the creator of the world"

---

* A crucial image corroborates the link of Raban's wish dream to Kafka's poetics. Kafka frequently uses the image of "draft" or "current" ("Zug") to denote inspiration. His work, he states, can succeed only "in ganzem Zug" (T 267), in a single complete uninterrupted "draft" or "breath." In the passage of his early letter to Oskar Pollak, which I quoted, he speaks of "lifting in one single draft (*Zug*) that which I think I have in me." (My translation of "Zug" by "heave" obscures the close relationship to Raban's fantasy.) In Raban's dream of omnipotence, a draft of air always blows through his room. This image associates Raban's dream with Kafka's precondition for successful writing.

(T 314). A fairly crass example of the desire for divine transfiguration by virtue of the creative act appears in a dream which Kafka jotted down in his diary. His "literary projects" come on "an enormous chariot," and naked girls resembling the houris of Islamic paradise lift the author upward from his earthly "wretchedness" while his hand commands peace. He feels "the frontiers of human efforts," "at the farthest verge of human endeavor" (D II, 41),[20]

> und [ich] mache auf meiner Höhe aus eigenem Antrieb und plötzlich mich überkommendem Geschick das Kunststück . . . indem ich mich langsam zurückbeuge—eben versucht der Himmel aufzubrechen, um einer mir geltenden Erscheinung Raum zu geben, aber er stockt—den Kopf und Oberkörper zwischen meinen Beinen durchziehe und allmählich *wieder* als gerader Mensch *auferstehe.* War es *die letzte Steigerung, die Menschen gegeben ist?* (T 383f.; italics mine)

His inspired art, his "Kunststück," literally leads to the artist's "resurrection," and even though Heaven fails to give the promised special sign to him, and the self-ironic stance is unmistakable, the hubris in this dream clearly alludes to a Faustian striving for the "ultimate" possibilities of man. In a late diary entry, Kafka sees his literary mission, which is born from "loneliness," as "an assault upon the ultimate frontier of earthly life." "This entire literature," by which, as the context makes clear, Kafka understands his own writing, could have "easily developed into a secret doctrine, a new cabala" (T 553). Indications for this he sees in his work. However, it is a superhuman task requiring an "unimaginable genius" with the ability to recreate the past and to create the future. We see here how the distant descendant of Kant's "aesthetic idea," which Kafka's visionary poetics represents, likewise entails the corollary to it—Kant's doctrine of trans-rational genius. In Kant's aesthetics the genius functions like another demiurge giving his own laws to the second nature he creates in his art. Similarly, Kafka finds that literature, as he conceives it, demands the strength and power of a demiurge of history. After *The Judgment*—a success that in Kafka's own eyes was never repeated—he increasingly felt that such strength was utterly wanting in himself. Far from imagining that he possessed the quasi-divine powers required for his mission, he considered himself in his diaries and letters the least adequate instrument for his task—sluggish, feeble, sickly, ill-equipped in body, in feeling, and in mind. Yet the demand persisted.

However, the gravest threat to this demand came from the nature of writing itself. Kafka's ideal was to give the most faithful expression to the truth within himself, and he thought he had achieved that in writing *The Judgment.* Such a faith seemed to justify all sacrifices. This faith required as its formal correlative the restriction of the narrative point of view to a single consciousness and the absence of an omniscient narrator interjecting himself between work and reader. According to Friedrich Beißner, this "unitary perspective" is the chief characteristic of Kafka's art in which its singular truthfulness resides.[21] Despite the profound modifications which Beißner's theory needs to become truly valid for Kafka's actual practice,[22] Kafka's literary judgments, as Hartmut Binder has shown,[23] tend to support Beißner's view. Kafka valued above all else the greatest possible closeness between the feelings of the fictional characters in a scene and those of the author in writing it. The union between writer and text, thus established, constituted for Kafka the truthfulness of the work, in which the reader would naturally share. Thus writing would bring about by a detour precisely that communication which speech had difficulty achieving, and without which the messianic ambitions of literature would have no basis.

However, after *The Judgment*, in the period of *The Trial*, Kafka began to realize that his writing was by no means a vehicle of the truth, but the opposite—an instrument of counterfeit. In looking back on "the best" he "had written" (T 448), he found that it derived its strength from duplicity. His best passages—according to him, always scenes of dying—were perfectly designed to fool the reader. Kafka enjoyed the dying of his protagonists and luxuriated in death scenes. His writing, however, masked his joy so completely that to the reader these scenes appeared terribly sad and deeply moving. By staying within the point of view of the protagonist, who viewed his death as "an injustice" or at least a harsh fate, the reader, made to identify with the character, shared his grievance, while the author savored "such descriptions secretly as a game":

> . . . ich freue mich ja in dem Sterbenden zu sterben, nütze daher mit Berechnung die auf den Tod gesammelte Aufmerksamkeit des Lesers aus, bin bei viel klarerem Verstande als er, von dem ich annehme, daß er auf dem Sterbebett klagen wird, und meine Klage ist daher möglichst vollkommen, bricht auch nicht etwa plötzlich ab wie wirkliche Klage, sondern verläuft schön und rein. Es ist so, wie ich der Mutter gegenüber immer über Leiden mich beklagte, die bei weitem nicht so groß waren, wie die Klage glauben ließ. Gegenüber der Mutter brauchte ich allerdings nicht so viel Kunstaufwand wie gegenüber dem Leser. (T 448f.)

Such artful deceit and clever contriving for aesthetic effect, while attesting to Kafka's subtle mastery of the art of fiction, glaringly contradict his ideal of the writer's absolute faithfulness to and unity with the feeling permeating his work, and embodied in his character. The bifurcation of perspectives of author and character, and thus of author and reader, gives the lie to the presence of the writer's "truth" in his text. Thus Kafka failed to find in his own work that indivisible unity between conception and execution which he demanded of literature. The mere restriction of the point of view to the protagonist does not, contrary to Beißner's claim, guarantee the truthfulness of the work. On the contrary, the apparent absence of an omniscient narrator only helps to hoodwink the reader all the more effectively by suggesting an identity between author and protagonist that is not there. The author in his concealment manipulates and dupes the reader who, one can easily imagine, might be horrified to learn that his "tears" were a calculated side effect of the author's sado-masochistic "play."

There is a striking parallelism between Kafka's literary strategy, as described in this diary entry, and the structure of Raban's dream. Both, first of all, are seen as infantile devices. Raban's split self was originally a child's fantasy, and Kafka compares his literary artifice to the child's device of exaggerating his ailments to get his mother's sympathy. The hidden author, in Kafka's diary entry, corresponds to Raban's inhuman truth. The dying fictional character parallels Raban's pretended human self, and the outside world that is taken in by Raban's human façade has its equivalent in Kafka's deceived reader. Ironically it is the very idea of a "true self" that spells out deception. Raban sends out his "stand-in" to fake his presence in human relationships from which he is "really" absent. Thus precisely by becoming his "truth," Raban cheats. His fantasy, if taken seriously and carried over into life, would entail emotional disaster for his dupes.

Duplicity, Kafka comes to recognize, is built into the very act of writing fiction, since in it the self inevitably splits into the writer and the character, or into the subject and the object of reflection. The "eigene Gestalt" is for Kafka the primary subject of literature, and remains for him the prototype of all fictional characters. But in this self-reflection the unity between the writer and the writing is ruptured. In fact, it can never truly come about, or, at any rate, it cannot be sustained for any length of time. For from the moment the writing reflects on the subject it writes about, the perfect congruence of writer and subject, which is truth, becomes impossible. In its place a playful and coquettish self-regard arises which for Kafka is the infernal opposite of truth:

> Und das Teuflische [am Schreiben] scheint mir sehr klar. Es ist die Eitelkeit und Genußsucht, die immerfort um die eigene oder auch um eine fremde Gestalt—die Bewegung vervielfältigt sich dann, es wird ein Sonnensystem der Eitelkeit—schwirrt und sie genießt. Was der naive Mensch sich manchmal wünscht: "Ich wollte sterben und sehn, wie man mich beweint," das verwirklicht ein solcher Schriftsteller fortwährend, er stirbt (oder er lebt nicht) und beweint sich fortwährend. (B 384f.)

Narcissism for Kafka is only the extreme and logical consequence of reflection, since it is the ultimate result of the separation from being, and thus from truth, which occurs in reflection. Multiplication of characters in the literary work does not change the self-reflection at its basis, but merely intensifies it. Since fictional characters are self-projections of the author in varying degrees, "vanity" simply becomes "a solar system" instead of being confined to a single star.

With other authors of the *Sprachkrise*, Kafka held to the superiority of being over thinking, immediacy over reflection. What he dreaded in writing was its mediate character, its referential nature, and separation from being. The inevitably metaphoric nature of writing, its inability to be what it speaks about, describes, or evokes, brought on his despair. Half a year before the letter to Max Brod, from which I just quoted, Kafka noted in his diary: "Die Unselbständigkeit des Schreibens, die Abhängigkeit von dem Dienstmädchen, das einheizt, von der Katze, die sich am Ofen wärmt, selbst vom armen alten Menschen, der sich wärmt. Alles dies sind selbständige, eigengesetzliche Verrichtungen, nur das Schreiben ist hilflos, wohnt nicht in sich selbst, ist Spaß und Verzweiflung" (T 551).

Kafka's view of writing as "a joke"makes the comparison of his work with a "game"—even a Wittgensteinian "language game"[24]—plausible as long as we realize that it applies to Kafka's "despair," not to his ideal. Writing seen as self-referential "play" of language signals the breakdown of his faith in his own work as the medium of the truth buried in him. Self-reflection capped that fraudulence which, as the diary entry about his death scenes shows, Kafka found inherent in the strategy of "fiction."

In the ideal of writing, as Kafka conceived it, the author should be nothing but the medium for what wants to be expressed; but self-reflection steps between the inspiration and the act, and dams up and pollutes the flow from within. The self-made object shuts out the vision of that "enormous world inside the head" that writing was to bring into view. Literature stifles that which the writer's word is to liberate. A book "must be the axe for the frozen sea within us," Kafka wrote at age twenty-one (B 28). Any other use of literature, so he felt all his life, was mere "decoration." To demand sacrifices for such a purpose was a sin against life. However, self-reflection, in which for Kafka the nature of fiction resides, separates the self from its inner world and prevents truth from appearing. It perpetuates "the frozen sea" within the self.

We return here to the paradox which underlies Kafka's "Rabanesque" poetics. This poetics attempts to unite two contradictory projects. While it aims at the dissolution of the self to "allow the deeper layers to come to the fore" (T 34), it also directs the writer toward extreme self-absorption. Its fundamental quest—lifting the inner world into language, and thus into articulated consciousness—also has the dream of the ego's magic and messianic omnipotence built into it. The radiant glimpse of that immense inner world, like the light from inside the law in the prison chaplain's legend in *The Trial*, can show itself only when the shadow of the self no longer impedes vision. Yet, and this is the paradox which denied Kafka "permanent satisfaction" with his works, self-regard was inseparable from art that conceived of itself as "a descent" (B 384) into the interior of the self. In terms of his own poetics, then, Kafka had to be what Walter Benjamin called him—"ein Gescheiterter."[25]

The poetics I have tried to investigate here cannot alone illuminate the peculiar impact and power of Kafka's writing. Even the impasse to which this poetics led him cannot be fully understood without the communal, collective, and universalist aspect which, in addition to the inward and subjective side that I have dwelt upon, marked Kafka's idea of "truth" and language. Furthermore, a strong desire for clarification and understanding—in the broadest sense, for self-preservation—runs side by side with the visionary element in his art. Only when these other concerns are investigated can we hope to do justice to Kafka's "poetics." The present essay must be considered merely a first step toward that objective.[26]

[1]Cf. Theodore Ziolkowski's "James Joyces Epiphanie und die Überwindung der empirischen Welt in der modernen deutschen Prosa," *Deutsche Vierteljahrsschrift für Literaturwissenschaft und Geistesgeschichte,* 35 (1961), p. 596.

[2]*Briefe 1902–1924.* Ed. Max Brod (S. Fischer Verlag Lizenzausgabe. New York: Schocken Books, 1958). Referred to as B.

[3]Quoted from Robert Musil, *Prosa, Dramen, späte Briefe.* Ed. Adolf Frisé (Hamburg: Rowohlt, 1957), p. 15.

[4]*Gesammelte Werke,* II (Berlin: S. Fischer, 1924), p. 180.

[5]*De la Grammatologie (*Paris: Les Editions de Minuit, 1967), p. 102.

[6]Cf. *Grammatology.* Translated by Gayatri Chakravorty Spivak (Baltimore and London: The Johns Hopkins University Press, 1976 [1974]), "Translator's Preface," p. xvi.

[7]Anthony Thorlby, in his stimulating essay, "Anti-Mimesis: Kafka and Wittgenstein," crassly contradicts Kafka's own poetics when he writes: "Kafka's stories illustrate the dreadful problem that language is something altogether different from what it says . . . " *(On Kafka: Semi-Centenary Perspectives.* Ed. Franz Kuna [London: Paul Elek, 1976], p. 74.) This is precisely what Kafka cannot accept. "Language games" in Wittgenstein's sense are radically inappropriate to the intensely "realistic" and literal-minded seriousness with which Kafka pursues "truth" by means of his writing.

[8]*Tagebücher 1910-23.* Ed. Max Brod (New York: Schocken Books, 1948 and 1949). Referred to as T.

[9]The close relationship between Kafka's writing and his dream life has frequently been noted. Cf. particularly S. Fraiberg, "Kafka and the Dream," *Partisan Review,* XXIII (1956), pp. 47-69; Michel Dentan, *Humour et création littéraire dans l'œuvre de Kafka* (Geneva / Paris: Librairie Droz / Librairie Minard, 1961), *passim*; Friedrich Altenhöner, *Der Traum und die Traumstruktur im Werk Franz Kafkas,* Diss. Münster 1962. Hartmut Binder has also pointed to the flood of visions that "crowded in" on Kafka so that he could consider "die Ausstoßung ins Kunstwerk als großes Glück" *(Motiv und Gestaltung bei Franz Kafka* [Bonn: Bouvier, 1966], p. 117). A systematic investigation and analysis of the visionary element in Kafka's work has not yet been undertaken.

[10]Cf. Walter H. Sokel, *Franz Kafka: Tragik und Ironie. Zur Struktur seiner Kunst* (Munich / Vienna: Albert Langen / Georg Müller, 1964).

[11]Cf. particularly the long explanatory letter, dated end of October / beginning of November 1914, and the very last letter to Felice, dated October 16, 1917.

[12]Cf. my *The Writer in Extremis: Expressionism in Twentieth-Century German Literature* (Stanford: Stanford University Press, 1959), p. 12.

[13]". . . unter einer ästhetischen Idee aber verstehe ich diejenige Vorstellung der Einbildungskraft, die viel zu denken veranlaßt, ohne daß ihr doch ein bestimmter Gedanke, d.i. *Begriff* adäquat sein kann, die folglich keine Sprache völlig erreicht und verständlich machen kann" (*Kritik der Urteilskraft,* § 49).

[14]Cf. *Briefe an Felice und andere Korrespondenz aus der Verlobungszeit.* Ed. Erich Heller und Jürgen Born. Lizenzausgabe von Schocken Books, New York (Fischer Verlag, 1967), pp. 394, 396 (hereafter referred to as BF). Side by side with the oneiric and fantastic tendency of Kafka's art, a strong rational current also runs through his work and forms a powerful complement to the visionary strain in it. His writing can be divided into two distinct types: visions and illustrations. The latter are similes or metaphors, serving basically explanatory purposes, and frequently extended into parabolic narratives. (Cf. particularly Karl-Heinz Fingerhut, *Die Funktion der Tierfiguren im Werke Franz Kafkas: Offene Erzählgerüste und Figurenspiele* [Bonn: H. Bouvier & Co., 1969], pp. 37-40, 45-59, and Hartmut Binder, *Kafka in neuer Sicht: Mimik, Gestik und Personengefüge als Darstellung des Autobiographischen* [Stuttgart: J.B. Metzler, 1976], pp. 7-20.) For the distinction between the two types of Kafka's narratives, see my "Das Verhältnis der Erzählperspektive zu Erzählgeschehen und Sinngehalt in 'Vor dem Gesetz,' 'Schakale und Araber' und 'Der Prozeß'," *Zeitschrift für deutsche Philologie,* 86 (1967), pp. 267-300. Stanley Corngold's trenchant essay—"The Structure of Kafka's Metamorphosis: Metamorphosis of the Metaphor"—denies the metaphoric nature of Kafka's art and claims that Kafka "is the writer par excellence who came to detect in metaphorical language a crucial obstacle to his own enterprise" (*The Commentator's Despair: The Interpretation of Kafka's 'Metamorphosis'* [Port Washington, New York / London: National University Publications Kennikat Press, 1973], p. 5). The present essay certainly agrees with Corngold's approach, and particularly with his assertion that "the desire to represent a state of mind directly in language, in a form consubstantial with that consciousness" (p. 7), was Kafka's avowed goal. However, as I shall try to show in a subsequent publication, Corngold does justice to only one aspect of Kafka's poetics and ignores other very powerful and contradictory intentions of his work.

[15]*Hochzeitsvorbereitungen auf dem Lande und andere Prosa aus dem Nachlaß.* Ed. Max Brod (New York: Schocken Books, 1953). This volume will hereafter be referred to as H.

[16]Binder points out that Kafka's last great fragment, "The Burrow," was, according to Dora Diamant, also written in one single night (Cf. *Motiv,* p. 118 and J.P. Hodin, "Erinnerungen an Franz Kafka," *Der Monat,* 9 [1949], pp. 8-9, 89-96.)

[17]*Über Franz Kafka* (Frankfurt: Fischer Taschenbuch Verlag, 1974), p. 114.

[18]Cf. Lionel Trilling, *Sincerity and Authenticity* (Cambridge, Massachusetts: Harvard University Press, 1971, 1972), *passim.*

[19]Corngold, p. 21.

[20]*The Diaries of Franz Kafka 1914-1923.* Ed. Max Brod. Translated by Martin Greenberg with the cooperation of Hannah Arendt. First Schocken Paperback Edition 1965 (New York: Schocken Books, 1974).

[21]Cf. Friedrich Beißner, *Der Erzähler Franz Kafka: Ein Vortrag* (Stuttgart: W. Kohlhammer, 1952).

[22]Cf. especially Klaus-Peter Philippi, *Reflexion und Wirklichkeit: Untersuchungen zu Kafkas Roman 'Das Schloß'* (Tübingen: Max Niemeyer Verlag, 1966), pp. 14-32.

[23]"Kafkas literarische Urteile," *Zeitschrift für deutsche Philologie,* 86 (1967), p. 230.

[24]Cf. Thorlby.

[25]"Um Kafkas Figur in ihrer Reinheit und in ihrer eigentümlichen Schönheit gerecht zu werden, darf man das Eine nie aus dem Auge lassen: es ist die von einem Gescheiterten." *Briefe.* Ed. Gershom Scholem and Theodor W. Adorno. Vol. 2 (Frankfurt: Suhrkamp, 1966), p. 764.

[26]This essay was first published in the journal of the International Arthur Schnitzler Research Association, *Modern Austrian Literature,* II, Nos. 3/4 (1978). Permission to reprint it here is gratefully acknowledged.

Varieties of Phonetic Poetry:
An Introduction

PETER DEMETZ

Our renewed consciousness of poesy carried by organized streams of sound has a long history in which times of the finest hearing alternate with epochs of the deaf ear. The Russian Formalists, more than fifty years ago, were certainly right in suggesting that friends of literature should be *ear*-rather than *eye*-people, and even if the Formalists in their time did not convince everybody of the necessity of listening to poetic sounds, our age of renascent semiotics, intent upon making important distinctions between visual and auditory signs, and perhaps the new grass-roots, communal, oral poetry, in this country as well as among the restive Soviet writers, have done much to change our encounters with poetic texts. We are aware again that we have to listen more carefully than we have in the past and, encouraged by the late Marshall McLuhan, if not by contemporary linguistics committed to analyzing everyday speech acts, we are less disturbed than previously by a growing suspicion that poetry or even literature at large, as something kept in the written or printed records, is but an island in oceans of oral communications. In my interest in modern phonetic poetry, in which sound more often than not prevails over meaning, I find myself in an ambivalent position. I am respectful of tradition, but am not a traditionalist entirely, and I am far from wanting to suggest that we should regress to the *Urschrei*, the primal scream, or to mere babble as the true source of poetry. Yet I do not want to close my ears to some recent experiments because I suspect that these articulations (in which our usual expectations of what a poem should be are ruthlessly counteracted) offer something we should know about the uneasy relationship of sound, meaning, and writing.

It was Roman Jakobson who (building on Karl Bühler's model) defined the different functions of language potentially present in any utterance and, by distinguishing between poetic and referential functions, as well as among a few others, made it less difficult for us to deal with what traditionalists may term mere "sound." He suggested that a self-concerned poetic utterance was characterized by withdrawal from the referential sphere, and made it more legitimate to bracket questions of imitation, reference, and denotation. In following his example, I do not want to revive issues of *l'art pour l'art*, but to emancipate questions of poetic discourse, at least for the

23

time being, from problems of social, philosophical, or metaphysical relevance, and, by narrowing our field of observation, I hope to sharpen our perception of the smallest parts. Keeping Jakobson's methodological assumptions in mind, we are free to postpone either/or decisions about some disturbing texts which we barely tolerate in our inherited canon of literature; and once we are courageous enough to assume that there may be an *imbalance* of functions in *all* utterances (Dada or not) we may be more willing to look at language experiments which radically *un*balance that which we believe to be proper balance, proportion, and integrity. We have to overcome our belief that verbal experiments are egotistic games played by poetic narcissists, and accept the possibility that in these challenges to our sensibilities poetic discourse wants to *show* and *tell* of what it consists.

The process of unbalancing operates in more than one way and involves the presence or absence of semantic, phonetic, and graphic qualities which are all of importance in constituting a literary text as a device to provoke and, perhaps, to control a reader's or listener's response. If I call the potential of meaning *logopoeia*, using Ezra Pound's term in a simplified way, that of sound *phonopoeia*, and that of visual shape, in writing or printing, *graphopoeia*, I assume that in a main-stream poem, as *e.g.* in Goethe's "Über allen Gipfeln ist Ruh" or Heine's "Mit deinen blauen Augen," there is an efficient alliance of all three elements that dominates the encounter of text and reader. I also believe that in certain moments of literary history, widely dispersed in time, particular texts are produced which may cease to be texts in the accepted sense of the term: a predominance of *phonopoeia* pushes the text into the realm of a-semantic sound or, as we would say metaphorically, of music; or the hegemony of *graphopoeia* changes the text, beyond the borderline between the arts, into a picture which we may or may not hang on our wall. In the absence of these experiments, our concepts of tradition are blind and incomplete, for it is precisely the disturbed balance and the emancipation of elements in pictorial and phonetic poetry which teaches us to perceive what kind of happy alliances are alive in those poems which do not challenge our assumptions any more. Only in encountering so-called nonsense poems, *e.g.* by Wassilij Kandinsky, Lewis Carroll, Paul Scheerbart (much admired by Walter Benjamin), or Kurt Schwitters, we suddenly realize how much we thirst for meaning; and only after we have observed how intense *phono-* or *graphopoeia* may change a text into a sound composition or a potential picture, we are sharply aware of the virtualities dominant in any utterance of poesy. Babble and doodle do offer potential enlightenment.

In saying that the process of unbalancing occurs in many centuries and in many literatures, I want to imply that I do not wish to see these imbalances as something exclusively modern, but merely prefer to deal with some more recent developments because they strike me as more radical and more revealing than what we may observe in the more distant past. There are, of

Oiaí laéa oía ssísialu
Ensúdio trésa súdio míschnumi
Ia lon stuáz
Brorr schjatt
Oiázo tsuígulu
Ua sésa masúo tülü

Ua sésa maschiató toró
Oi séngu gádse ándola
Oi ándo séngu
Séngu ándola
Oi séngu
Gádse

Ina
Leíola
Kbaó
Sagór
Kadó
Kadó mai tiúsi
Suíjo ángola . . .

Blümner's "Ango Laina" is a poem that wants to communicate feelings, not meanings, in an absolute way: that is, free of all *logopoeic* burdens, references, and potential denotations. We have to admit that Blümner is very careful not to include any sound strings reminiscent of Latin or Greek, as Ball does on occasion, for instance in his "Labadas Gesang an die Wolken," or morphemes suggesting particular inflections. Another example to clarify the point: If Rudolf Carnap, in his *Logical Syntax of Language*, uses a sentence of invented words, "Pirots karulize elatically," we are still tempted, as Jakobson remarked, to think of the "pirots" (whatever they are) as something in the plural, and to believe that a single "pirot," whatever it, she, he is, "karulizes" because we find familiar signs of inflection. Yet I wonder whether it is possible to communicate without shaping sounds in a characteristic way set by the habits of a particular *parole*. We do not know much about Blümner's technique of recitation, but I suspect that he articulated his sounds as a native speaker born in Berlin, and trained in German theater elocution; dreaming of an absolute language, he was, as soon as he articulated aloud, incapable of going beyond the phonetic barrier inherent in his speech habits and, inventing sound strings of unheard-of courage, did not escape the prison of his set ways of, *e.g.*, pronouncing the long *u* in the German way.

But that is not all. I think he was a captive of his native German in a more paradoxical way, and I suspect that his emancipated sound actually responded to the inherited German sound structure in the manner of a dialectical inversion. He wants to go as far as possible beyond all German sound configurations, and yet, because he wants systematically to avoid the usual German distribution of sounds, he creates new patterns which are indirectly defined by the structures he wants to oppose in his ear and in our hearing. A statistical analysis of sound distribution in modern spoken German would clearly indicate that the unstressed *e*, as in the second syllables of *geben, leben, reden,* recurs most often among all German speech sounds (11.95%), and if other variants are added, the index increases to 17.66%. It is revealing that such an unstressed *e*, the most characteristic of all German sounds, does not appear in Blümner's poem once. But there are other indications that Blümner's "skew," or pattern of sound distribution, is designed radically to negate the traditional sound patterns of his native tongue. The sequence "unstressed *e + n*" present in nearly 5% of all German sound strings, does not appear either, and the German "skew" of vowels and liquids is nearly reversed in Blümner's idiom. He avoids most *Umlaute*, dramatically increases the recurrence of long stressed *o*, which in his native tongue provides a mere 0.86% of all sound materials, and in a striking way increases the occurrence of *l* which in German figures only in the middle ranks (4.25%) between *n* (9.32) and *p* (1.2). These sound statistics, however unusual in discussions of poetry, are helpful in suggesting that Blümner, in developing his absolute language, really works with a statistical "skew" of sounds *against* German, as something to be opposed, to be argued against. Spoken German is the auditory ground against which Blümner's absolute idiom operates, and, as a sound poet, he reminds me of one of those atheists who cannot explain what they really believe unless they discuss the entire history of theology.

It is perhaps little known that Blümner was among those writers and art critics who convinced Kurt Schwitters to experiment with colors and sound, rather than to cultivate what he had learned at the Dresden Academy. Blümner recited his poetry in Hanover in the fall of 1918, and the young graphic artist and writer Schwitters, who was among his listeners, began to experiment himself and, within a year or two, was as radical as anybody among the *Sturm* people or the Dadaists in Zurich and Berlin. In the United States, Schwitters is known as the ingenious and witty master of collage, but his many and variegated verbal experiments are far less known; the trouble with him is, of course, that he was a totally unorthodox and playful artist who happily let the hundred flowers of his talents bloom. Early and late in his life, he painted old fashioned landscapes and traditional portraits while, at the same time, competing with the Russian and Dutch Constructivists in brilliance and courage of graphic experiments; and in his literary work he was equally willing to write funny fairy tales, charming nonsense verse, or to engage in the most ruthless and witty experiments with syntax or sound. I should like to concentrate on Schwitters' much disputed text "Wand":

Fünf Vier Drei Zwei Eins
Wand
Wand
WAND
WAND WAND WAND
WAND WAND WAND
WAND   WAND   WAND   WAND
wände
wände
Wände
WÄNDE WÄNDE WÄNDE
WÄNDE WÄNDE WÄNDE WÄNDE

WAND

WAND   WAND   WAND
WAND WAND WAND
wand   wand   wand
wand
wand
wand

wand

Schwitters himself would have said that his poem belongs to his "konse-quente Dichtung" in which he explores what he terms "internal rhythm," the constituent basis of all works of art. The actual text starts, after a count-down or blast-off line, with the rocket-like propulsion of a single word or, rather, its recurrence regulated by three organizational principles. There is, first, the morphological distinction between the singular "Wand" and the plural "Wände"; second, the intervals within the sequence of articulations, and, finally, the force of articulation, indicated by different graphemes sug-gesting (I think) a *piano, mezzoforte,* and *forte* level of voice. The semantic charge amounts to a minimum, but there is a complex and sophisticated or-ganization of the morphological signals, the presence/absence of the contin-uous sound stream, and the changing intensity of voice; and if I listen care-fully to the sound string, I may discover that the text operates with proportions and symmetries which can be formalized in a numerical way. Morphologically, the text offers, in its central part, 10 plurals of the basic element, surrounded, or preceded and followed, by 13 singulars (the coda echoes the title); and concentrating on the indications of sound level, I would say that the text forms three parts in which the first and second prompt me to read with ascending pitch while in the third part my voice descends. The point is that from the collaboration of sounds, intonations, and intensi-ties an intricate and attractive experience of our aural sensibility results which refuses to yield sense in a traditional way.

Critics have had considerable difficulties with Schwitters' "Wand," and interpretations (if it is possible to speak about hermeneutic efforts) have ranged, in my experience, from the assertion that the text, as a performative act, builds up a wall of sounds, to the helpless suggestion that we are in the presence of one of those Dada jokes which do not merit closer attention whatsoever. I take the joke as seriously as Schwitters who, as a verbal and graphic artist, was very much concerned with fundamental questions of art, and I submit that in "Wand" he wants to test the possibility of creating a verbal structure which would have all the organizational characteristics of a highly structured field of formal interrelationships, except that of making sense. "Wand" may be an experiment crossing the boundaries between the arts, yet it derives its considerable charm from Schwitters' attempt to transfer insights about the composition of a graphic art work to literature, or, to be more precise, from his abstractions in the graphic arts to poetic discourse. In the early 1920's the industrial designer Schwitters came to the conclusion that a work of art, in order to be one, had to fulfill two basic requirements—the requirement of showing an "internal rhythm," that is, a rich and intricate interrelationship of parts with each other, and the requirement of being isolated by a *découpage*, a cut, a line, a threshold, or a white space from surrounding sensory experience which does not show an equally high degree of formal organization. He suggests that any work of art consists of an "internal rhythm" disengaged from the surrounding experience of a lesser structure—the problem is, however, that such an "internal rhythm" (the idea of which Schwitters derived from Herwarth Walden's articles about expressionist painting) functions differently in the different systems of the graphic and the verbal arts; and while shifting his ideas and his terms from speaking about his collages to verbal experimentation, Schwitters creates revealing difficulties for his readers/listeners because he assumes that words which have lexical meanings can be used, within disengaged fields of formal intricacy, as if they did not carry with them a resilient power of semantic direction at all. Schwitters leaves us productively puzzled by the question of whether the internal patterns of "Wand" actually enhance or diminish the semantic load of the basic material; and if it is diminished or perhaps destroyed, we are challenged by the further question of whether there can be verbal art constituted by an intentional lack of sense, and yet of a significance of another kind.

Schwitters' Viennese friend Raoul Hausmann had particular reasons for misunderstanding Schwitters' texts because he had long developed radical "soundings" of his own which sound as if they were to end all sound poetry. Hausmann (who survived the Nazis by hiding in Southern France) went so far in his ruthless negation of any establishment, mainstream *or* avantgarde, as to find himself in fierce opposition against the Expressionists, the *Sturm* people, and the Dadaists, declaring in his many manifestoes that the best Dada was *anti-dadaist*—negation itself had to be negated again and again. Hausmann, as did Ball and Schwitters, recited his texts publicly, to shock his audiences; and while we have the texts of some of his theoretical writings, we do not have many scores of his sound performances. I offer here a notation from one of them:

```
K P' E R I    U M    L P' E R I O U M
N M' P E R I I I      pernoumum
bpretiberrerrebee    onnoooooooooh    gplanpouk
komnpout        perikoul
rreeeeeEEErreeeee            A
oapderree    mglepadonou    mtnou
            tnoumt
```

We do not have many scores because Hausmann rarely intended to transform his sounds into graphemes; in striking contrast to Schwitters, who works on his sound texts with great care and uses many signs usually found in musical scores, Hausmann never bothered systematically to preserve his recitations in print. Perhaps I should say that while seemingly belonging to the early phonetic poets of our century, he was not really one of them; to him, I suspect, it was not the sound and the sound strings that mattered but only the way in which the sounds were produced by the human apparatus of articulation. Ultimately it was not the phonetic element which was of concern to him, but the exercise of the articulatory motor impulse in a physiological sense.

We have at least some indication in one of his confusing Dada manifestoes about the "Legitimacy of Sound" (1921) which, in pretending to oppose traditional essays by speaking nonsense, nevertheless suggests something of the ideas which he had in mind. He does not speak about sounds at all, but about the relationship or, rather, the analogies that obtain between art and smoking—what art and smoking have in common is the fact that they create a moment of "serenity as such in the infantile behavior of life," offering us, in the middle of hectic experience, the "consoling certainty of the uniqueness of what happens" (when we meditate on art or smoke a cigarette, leisurely inhaling and exhaling the air). Hausmann speaks a good deal about *Navy-cut* tobacco but deals with smoking as a convenient metaphor; to him, smoking is a productive emblem of how breathing is disciplined in a recurrent rhythm, and it is the willed act of breathing which is of central interest. We are immersed in a unique moment in which all virtualities of life are gathered, our social alienation is negated, and we feel in a nearly mystical way that we are liberated from the confinements of time and space. I am speaking of a nearly mystical experience because Hausmann himself pushes us in that direction; in his manifesto, he alludes to the *Prana* ("wisdom") and the *Tattwa* (force field of change), and the presence of these terms, ultimately derived from the old religions of India, reveals the full implications of what he wishes to say. Smoking stands here for the exercise of breathing, and breathing for the exercise of motor energy in producing sound by pushing a stream of air past and against particular obstructions in the upper part of our body— what we achieve when we exercise our physiological powers is that we release energy and approach a moment of unique serenity which takes us out of a world of intolerable pressures. I suspect that what is called Hausmann's "sound poetry" is but a sediment of his articulatory exercises which, as activating energy, are far more important than what they actually produce; and even if Hausmann may have a rather fragmentary knowledge of Yoga, he is well on his way to longing for a spiritual *Mantra* to guide and govern life. What he recites may sound like phonetic poetry, but I think that we are moving towards motor exercises, into a realm of therapy using the healing release of body energy.

Most of my examples of sound poetry have been selected from experiments of the productive years 1916 to 1921, and another essay would be needed to discuss the resuscitation of phonetic poetry after the hiatus of the war years and the transformations of sound poetry by electronic hardware after the mid-1950's. I have been tempted to deal with sound problems from a perspective of synchrony, but I think I know what I had to ignore and to sacrifice. Much of a theory of phonetic poetry, as far as the relationship of sound and meaning is concerned, develops together with semiotics and the philosophy of language in Plato's *Cratylos*, in Stoic logic, in Locke and Leibniz; and a critical analysis of these problems in historical perspective would not neglect to discuss Jacob Böhme's language speculations (recently analyzed by Steve Konopacki) and the sound experiments of the international Baroque. Yet I believe that our modern concerns with what language can do, and what the materials of poetic discourse are, have pushed us to more radical insights and demands; and we have yet to analyze dispassionately how it happened and what it implies that the posthumous publication of de Saussure's *Introduction to General Linguistics* in 1916 coincides with the first Dada manifestoes in Zurich, very much concerned with language, and the question of public and private meaning.

Listening to phonetic poetry, even of a particular period in history, challenges our aesthetic habits, I think, in very important and productive ways. We are less certain, after listening to Schwitters, that a close collaboration of sound, writing, and meaning is an absolute, necessary, and unchangeable condition of poetry, and we begin to suspect that the functional togetherness of *logopoeia, phonopoeia,* and *graphopoeia,* which is characteristic of the central body of our literary tradition, may be close to being another social convention, brittle, unstable, and fragile, rather than something given by nature once and for all. But there are other challenges of a social and aesthetic kind. In the texts of Ball and Blümner, our options concerning ethics and language are at stake because these writers are desperately concerned with rescuing what they believe to be the absolute purity of language, outside their infected and diseased native tongue, or any natural tongue if it cannot be done otherwise, and we have to ask ourselves whether they do not confuse the system of *language* with the particular ways in which individual speakers actually behave (I remember many people of my generation who in exile refused to speak or write German because they believed that, somehow, the language itself was sick). Kurt Schwitters provokes our ontological ideas about how works of art exist; and while he organizes his patterns and rhythms of whatever materials, sound among them, he really asks the question whether meaning is among the essential or peripheral necessities of art. Hausmann pushes his experiments beyond the confines of literature to anthropology or physiotherapy; exploring the physiological circumstances of human articulation, he moves into a space in which questions of meaning and writing are totally irrelevant, and we are asked whether we can achieve a healing moment of serenity by employing our organs of sound articulation.

Yet I would like to place my discussion of sound and meaning in the wider context of the present moment, and I am asking myself whether these questions are not also relevant in view of Susan Sontag's demand that we need an erotics, not a hermeneutics, of art—that is, that we should be eager to feel the sensual pleasures yielded by art, rather than to exert our energies in the hermeneutic search for meaning. Considering the inclinations and predilections of our contemporary discussions of literature, largely dominated by the friends and adversaries of Hirsch, Gadamer, or Derrida, I suspect that we are committed once again to assuming that poems are philosophical or theological statements of sorts. We grapple with the potential presence or absence of meaning, and totally neglect, underrate, or forget that the idiom of poetry, if it is that of poetry, has a sensual quality that, unlike philosophical assertion (whether or not under deconstructionist "erasure"), directly affects us as human beings who touch and feel. Phonetic poetry undoes balances within the poem but restores balances of a humane kind. We may be hermeneutic animals who cannot live without meaning, but it is the ultimate challenge of sound experiments to remind us that in a particular discourse called poetry there is something that has to strike our senses before making sense.

Confessions of a Poet:
Poetry and Politics in Brecht's Lyric

REINHOLD GRIMM

Ausschließlich wegen der zunehmenden Unordnung
In unseren Städten des Klassenkampfs
Haben etliche von uns in diesen Jahren beschlossen
Nicht mehr zu reden von Hafenstädten, Schnee auf den Dächern, Frauen
Geruch reifer Äpfel im Keller, Empfindungen des Fleisches
All dem, was den Menschen rund macht und menschlich
Sondern zu reden nur mehr von der Unordnung
Also einseitig zu werden, dürr, verstrickt in die Geschäfte
Der Politik und das trockene, "unwürdige" Vokabular
Der dialektischen Ökonomie
Damit nicht dieses furchtbare gedrängte Zusammensein
Von Schneefällen (sie sind nicht nur kalt, wir wissen's)
Ausbeutung, verlocktem Fleisch und Klassenjustiz eine Billigung
So vielseitiger Welt in uns erzeuge, Lust an
Den Widersprüchen solch blutigen Lebens
Ihr versteht. (9, 519)*

Do away with art? Oh no! Bertolt Brecht does not want to do that. He
has no intention of nullifying art—despite all such "confessions." It
should—*it must*—exist! Never, not even in these verses from his exile—lines
which sound so much of dismissal and finality—did Brecht repudiate art. It
must exist, even if it seems to be criminal and wanton to us, a blatant injustice and impossibility! Man still acts like a wolf toward his fellow men; every-
where, as in times past, men, classes, entire peoples and continents are being
enslaved, exploited, and ground to dust; today more than ever a brutish humanity, oppressed and oppressor at the same time, threatens to choke on its
own bloody swill. And yet, in spite of everything, art must be. Even "pure"
art in the midst of our dark era, as none other than the political poet Brecht
confided to us.

For precisely Brecht, the poet who, without any reservation, considered his work to be a fight for the liberation of the exploited and oppressed,
the disenfranchised and degraded, the demeaned and defamed: he also
spoke in behalf of art, even of "pure" art. Precisely he who placed himself

* All references in the text are to Bertolt Brecht, *Gesammelte Werke in 20 Bänden*
(Frankfurt: Suhrkamp, 1967). Copyright © 1964 by Stefan S. Brecht. Permission to quote them
here is gratefully acknowledged.

totally in the service of the humanization of humanity, desired that art exists. Even by denying it he declared himself for it. He who "solely because of the increasing disorder"—what an immoderate moderation—seems once and for all to forswear any kind of aesthetic pleasure, does this through the medium of art, as a poet, in verse and accomplished, masterfully manipulated language. And there is more yet. He who makes such protestations to us, who from now on intends to employ art "only" as a weapon, expressly and unequivocally professed aesthetic pleasure—indeed at approximately the same time! In Brecht's posthumously published *Me-ti*, his collection of dialectical-didactic prose in the style of the ancient Chinese, there is a text which has an almost more muted and restrained effect than our poem but which is, nonetheless, scarcely less striking. For this short piece of prose— allegory or aphoristic parable, yet quite realistic—bears the titel "Über reine Kunst."

But let's listen to Brecht's confession! Let's hear what Me-ti, the political philosopher, has to relate about Kin-jeh, the political poet:

> Me-ti sagte: Neulich fragte mich der Dichter Kin-jeh, ob er in diesen Zeitläuften Gedichte über Naturstimmungen schreiben dürfe. Ich antwortete ihm: Ja. Als ich ihn wieder traf, fragte ich ihn, ob er Gedichte über Naturstimmungen geschrieben habe. Er antwortete: Nein. Warum, fragte ich. Er sagte: Ich stellte mir die Aufgabe, das Geräusch fallender Regentropfen zu einem genußvollen Erlebnis des Lesers zu machen. Darüber nachdenkend und hie und da eine Zeile skizzierend, erkannte ich es als nötig, dieses Geräusch fallender Regentropfen für alle Menschen, also auch für solche Menschen zu einem genußvollen Erlebnis zu machen, die kein Obdach besitzen und denen die Tropfen zwischen Kragen und Hals fallen, während sie zu schlafen versuchen. Vor dieser Aufgabe schreckte ich zurück.
>
> Die Kunst rechnet nicht nur mit dem heutigen Tag, sagte ich versucherisch. Da es immer solche Regentropfen geben wird, könnte ein Gedicht dieser Art lange dauern. Ja, sagte er traurig, wenn es keine solche Menschen mehr geben wird, denen sie zwischen Kragen und Hals fallen, kann es geschrieben werden. (12, 509)

Not only a utopian dimension makes this bit of prose stand out, but also a historical one. For, while Kin-jeh is a fictional figure, Me-ti is one from history. He was a dialectician and "socio-moral philosopher" who lived over two and a half millenia ago as a contemporary and ideological rival of Confucius. Once again, as he did so often, Brecht has slipped on a poetical garment in order to "emerge through real sleeves."Just as little as his choice of two figures can their Chinese disguise deceive us about the confessional aspect of his text. The philosophical dialectician Me-ti is just as much Brecht's *alter ego* as the dialectical lyricist Kin-jeh. At the turn in their conversation ("I shrank back" / "I said temptingly") both, in eloquent silence, indiscernibly blend together. That which "On Pure Art" accomplishes is the same topicality which we already encountered in Brecht's verses. Neither the glimmering of a distant future nor the shadows of the past can conceal this burning present.

To be sure, while in the poem an intensely afflicted ego accounts to us and posterity, in the prose text it conducts a dialogue with itself. But the confessions are the same. Once again they are: "Pure" lyric poetry can and may not be written nowadays. Even lines which merely deal with "the sound of falling raindrops" (or, for that matter, the "smell of ripe apples in the cellar," the sight of "snow on roofs"): these, too, are denied the poet. Indeed, with the awareness of destitution and despair, such sensual writing and reading is not simply despised and prohibited—it is, in view of our "bloody world" with its "awful cramped coexistence" of the naturally beautiful with human injustice and misery, absolutely immoral. Ethics and aesthetics appear irreconcilable, the social and artistic conscience agonizingly divided, as long as those daintily splashing raindrops run down the necks of the homeless and that innocent snow ("not only cold" but also an ancient symbol of purity, as "we know") gleams merrily from the roof-tops after it has covered up the cadavers of the frozen—mercifully, as many a poet maintains. And who cares about the smell of apples in the cool, roomy cellars of the rich when elsewhere in the stinking pits of poverty children starve and the sick perish? "Before this task"—again what an immoderate moderation—the poet, both times, "shrank back." In Brecht's verse as well as in his prose piece, art—at least as "pure art"—has become impossible; all that remains is "art as weapon" and with it the painful decision of estrangement and renunciation in order, as he says with the utmost objectivity and austerity, "to become one-sided, reduced, enmeshed in the business of politics and the dry "indecorous" vocabulary of dialectical economics . . . " Indeed, the lyrical ego and its epic counterparts confess the same thing to us. The only difference between them is apparently that the decision which does not emerge until the end of the parable is clearly and irrevocably pronounced in the poem. Yet had not Kin-jeh in mute conversation with Me-ti already decreed what Brecht's poem bluntly expresses? Just as, on the other hand, Brecht's poem, although it never mentions "art," let alone "pure art," constantly and unmistakably means precisely this?

Impossible to ignore, however, is that which Kin-jeh proclaims, not to say promises, both himself and us, and not merely between the lines but directly, even if somewhat "sadly." For someday, this he knows for sure, someday "it can be written," although not by him as he fears: that poem about the rain, the snow, and the smell of ripe apples in the cellar, that poem about "cities by the sea," "women," and the sensations "of the flesh," and thus about "all that makes a man round and human." One day, Brecht knows, man will no longer act as a wolf toward his fellow men, but will finally be a "helper." One day, sometime in the future, this humane work of art will, indeed must, be created. Even if in "somber eras," before the time is ripe, ethics and aesthetics are completely irreconcilable, they can—they *must*—be reconciled. The promise is more than just a promise: it is an unalterable demand. Brecht's and Kin-jeh's perception, their uneasy insight into the immorality of pure art today, reveals itself as an ethical postulate. For the less any art may now be possible, all the more so will it be then, in days to come—and precisely as "pure" art, seemingly superfluous and ostensibly non-essential though indispensable as a pleasurable, even joyful human experience. Art should and must exist, according to Kin-jeh as well as to Brecht.

And yet—or at least so it seems—there is still a considerable difference between them. Does not Kin-jeh look primarily into the future, whereas Brecht's lyrical ego gazes into the past? Does not the former speak of an art which cannot yet be and the latter of one which can no longer exist? Is not the somber renunciation of art in our inhumane present the only thing both have in common? But should that be the complete and ultimate answer of Brecht? If art is only present by its absence—doesn't this also mean that it either has, or can gain, presence precisely because it *is* absent? Isn't this the actual, the secret "Testament" of the early admirer of Villon, Bertolt Brecht? Not without reason have I frequently quoted from one of Brecht's most famous poems from the thirties, "An die Nachgeborenen." For here too, in this impressive and truly "Great Testament," the poet, in the midst of political strife, is concerned with nature and the "impressions of nature." And again, in addition to the sensations of the flesh and of love, they represent the human as well as artistic realm. To be sure, there is no longer any mention of pleasure, let alone joyful pleasure. On the contrary, Brecht laconically confides to us:

> Der Liebe pflegte ich achtlos
> Und die Natur sah ich ohne Geduld. (9, 724)

But was he completely "careless?" Completely "without patience?" No matter, just as in the bitter lines of his supposed *adieu* from art (lines which themselves are so artistic), the poet of humanity once again—and right in the province of art itself—experiences the essence of humanity with a bad conscience. And just as in his oriental prose dialogue, so here, too, does the nature poem, the lyric of pure feeling, serve him as a decisive paradigm. The most famous lines from that celebrated elegy are, as is well known, those in which Brecht forbids himself as well as us who, alas, are still his contemporaries although "born later," even a "harmless talk about trees" ("Gespräch über Bäume"). Or rather, "almost" forbids or would like to forbid:

> Was sind das für Zeiten, wo
> Ein Gespräch über Bäume fast ein Verbrechen ist
> Weil es ein Schweigen über so viele Untaten einschließt! (9, 723)

Such verses are, with all restraint, one single scream. May one at all, Brecht asks through Kin-jeh, "write poems about the impressions of nature in these times?" In the midst of this "bloody muddle," this "disorder" of a "dehumanized humanity," this "world which is like a slaughterhouse?" Then must one not disavow, proscribe, and banish from the present, at least the indirect experiences of the human, the round, and the beautiful if we cannot affect the direct ones? Must one not renounce, however reluctantly, every artistic creation today, every enhancement and alleviation of life through art? Brecht as well as Kin-jeh drew this conclusion, painful though it must have been for them. In fact, the poet drew it repeatedly: "solely because of the increasing disorder" and the "awful cramped coexistence." He also draws it, no less poignantly, in "To Those Born Later." But are not his words accomplished language, completely flawless poetry? Did he not once again create art, even while agonizingly negating it? Indeed, are we not tempted— "almost" tempted—to say, "pure" art?

Further, let us not forget that Me-ti, that "tempting" ego in Brecht's parable, answered Kin-jeh's question in the affirmative! And his answer, too, has weight. It cannot be flatly dismissed as irony (although I admit that there is some ironic resonance in it). That which Me-ti has decided about art is recanted no more than that which not only Brecht but "some of us," as he says, "have now decided." Art and the turning away from art, enjoyment of art and uncompromising morality, pleasure and asceticism exist side by side in Brecht—indeed, they merge. The poet did not simply find himself *between* two modes or periods of art, the older of which should no longer exist and the newer of which should not yet come into existence; he is not merely languishing in a hell equidistant from Paradise Lost as well as Paradise Regained. (Those are his images, by the way, not mine; in *Der gute Mensch von Sezuan* a character sings, "Am Sankt Nimmerleinstag / Wird die Erde zum Paradies," and in the same play Brecht exclaims, "Die Zeiten sind furchtbar, diese Stadt ist eine Hölle" [4, 1562, 1546].) Moreover, Brecht is not only concerned with such kinds of insights or decisions and their manifestations in a politically clear as well as poetically masterful manner. Neither is of importance to Me-ti, Brecht's other *alter ego*. In his text we read, "art does not only have to do with the present day"; and analogously, "since such [impressions of nature and pleasurable artistic experiences] will always exist, a poem of this kind could have a long existence." Thus speaks the advocate of "pure art." And is he not right, too? Is not his reply (the reply of the political philosopher) part and parcel of Brecht's ultimate answer? Not one jot of it is recanted by him.

To be sure, Brecht faced the beauty of nature without much devotion or fond lingering. But he did "see" it. His fleeting, nearly grudging—indeed, almost guilty—look did perceive things of nature: some part of their beauty, however little, remained fixed in his gaze and was transferred into some of his poems, even if merely as a negation. They are, in the truest sense of the word, precious lines, as one used to say in days gone by—and who knows, as one may someday say again. Even the "talk about trees" and what it implies, Brecht's "silence about so many horrors"—a silence, I might add, which was never his since he ceaselessly raised his voice against injustice—even such hopelessly gaping contrasts do not confront one another either absolutely or abruptly. After all, the poetical conversation is only "almost a crime"; and from the often forced, but nonetheless consistently broken political silence emanate not only the loathing for the hangmen and the bitterness about the victims, but also "red anger" and dismay about the innumerable atrocities. For like pure art, the Brechtian nature, again acting as a proxy for everything "that makes a man round and human," also achieves presence precisely through its absence. Nothing less than its elimination attests to its permanence. Again one could think of one of the great French writers, namely Stéphane Mallarmé—whom Brecht didn't exactly venerate, but with whose work he was quite familiar. Only by being denied a reality, and removed from a present state into an absent one, so Mallarmé claims, do things become completely real and achieve definitive presence as (pure) speech and (pure) art. *Une élévation ordinaire verse l'absence.*[1] "Absence," but also—as I deliberately translate—"a mere elevation." Or as Hugo Friedrich writes: "These renounced things have a presence solely in language, as art." Mallarmé's is a "poetry of negatives." In it, "that which is objectively eliminated by means of the language which states its absence, receives its spiritual existence in the selfsame language through its naming."[2] The correspondences with Brecht cannot be overlooked. But in his case, that of the political poet, they have as little to do with *poésie pure* as any *littérature engagée* is to be found in the Symbolist Mallarmé. Mallarmé's ethics were to the same degree aesthetic as Brecht's aesthetics were ethical.

Nonetheless, art and morality as well as nature and history are also reconcilable "in these times," and not merely in some distant future. In fact, they are already reconciled despite their contradictions—even in Bertolt Brecht. And the more permanently and agonizingly Brecht experienced those contradictions, the more relentlessly he witnessed and absorbed into his poetry those things that make a man evil and inhuman. Yes, this passionate poet of humanity as well as of class struggle knew more than most people of the personal menace growing out of such a struggle. Brecht proclaimed it (think of his play, *Die Maßnahme*) without any reservation:

> Auch der Haß gegen die Niedrigkeit
> Verzerrt die Züge.
> Auch der Zorn über das Unrecht
> Macht die Stimme heiser. Ach, wir
> Die wir den Boden bereiten wollten für Freundlichkeit
> Konnten selber nicht freundlich sein. (9, 725)

The more directly the poet speaks, the more grippingly he stirs us. Brecht's lament from exile when he was "changing countries more often than shoes" and nearly despairing has, therefore, and with good reason, long been one of his most famous poems. But no less gripping, one could say shattering, are the few lines which he wrote "solely because of the increasing disorder." For this most sparse and austere of his confessions—just one sentence—is at the same time the most pitiless and immeasurably open one. If one "understands" it correctly, as the poet pleads, then it surpasses even his "elegy."

That such verses are not only possible, but indispensable, bears overwhelming witness to the power of poetry, the "necessity of art."[3] And precisely that and how the innocently natural, mired in the sorrow, guilt, and entanglements of history, is taken up and thereby preserved in them is what makes them irrefutable affirmations of Brechtian lyric as well as of poetry in general. But as unique as they seem, they are not isolated phenomena within the context of Brecht's *œuvre*. For he has a whole series of poems in which the denial of the lyrical is itself transformed into the purest lyrical expression. Their very titles speak eloquently: "In finsteren Zeiten," "Schlechte Zeit für Lyrik," "Die Landschaft des Exils." And there are many more. "In Dark Times" offers perhaps the best example of that "evocation through negation," at least as far as technique and linguistic skill are concerned. Three times the poet begins with an express negation; three times he says expressly, "They won't say . . . " What follows, however, are precisely those "impressions of nature," those sensations "of the flesh" about which he no longer wanted to speak, which he really would have preferred to deny himself as well as us. But it is through this very process that they are confirmed: the wind in the trees; the summer day at the shore; the woman who softly enters the room. Just as indicative, of course, is also the sudden shift at the end of the poem:

> Man wird nicht sagen: Als da der Nußbaum sich im Wind schüttelte
> Sondern: Als der Anstreicher die Arbeiter niedertrat.
> Man wird nicht sagen: Als das Kind den flachen Kiesel über die Stromschnelle
> springen ließ
> Sondern: Als da die großen Kriege vorbereitet wurden.
> Man wird nicht sagen: Als da die Frau ins Zimmer kam
> Sondern: Als da die großen Mächte sich gegen die Arbeiter verbündeten.
> Aber man wird nicht sagen: Die Zeiten waren finster
> Sondern: Warum haben ihre Dichter geschwiegen? (9, 587)

Time and again, right down to the choice of words, we are confronted with the contrast between Brecht's "talk about trees" and his vocal "silence about so many atrocities." The fact that Hitler is not directly named but appears scornfully as the "house painter" (*der Anstreicher*) should not confuse us. Verses of this kind are, as nature poetry, masterpieces of a poetry of silence and yet, even more so, uncompromising political poetry.

Especially in poems from the Danish exile, one encounters such verses. The lyrical trilogy, "Frühling 1938," contains some of the most impressive examples:

I
Heute, Ostersonntag früh
Ging ein plötzlicher Schneesturm über die Insel.
Zwischen den grünenden Hecken lag Schnee. Mein junger Sohn
Holte mich zu einem Aprikosenbäumchen an der Hausmauer
Von einem Vers weg, in dem ich auf diejenigen mit dem Finger deutete
Die einen Krieg vorbereiteten, der
Den Kontinent, diese Insel, mein Volk, meine Familie und mich
Vertilgen mag. Schweigend
Legten wir einen Sack
Über den frierenden Baum.

II
Über dem Sund hängt Regengewölke, aber den Garten
Vergoldet noch die Sonne. Die Birnbäume
Haben grüne Blätter und noch keine Blüten, die Kirschbäume hingegen
Blüten und noch keine Blätter. Die weißen Dolden
Scheinen aus dürren Ästen zu sprießen.
Über das gekräuselte Sundwasser
Läuft ein kleines Boot mit geflicktem Segel.
In das Gezwitscher der Stare
Mischt sich der ferne Donner
Der manövrierenden Schiffsgeschütze
Des Dritten Reiches.

III
In den Weiden am Sund
Ruft in diesen Frühjahrsnächten oft das Käuzlein.
Nach dem Aberglauben der Bauern
Setzt das Käuzlein die Menschen davon in Kenntnis
Daß sie nicht lang leben. Mich
Der ich weiß, daß ich die Wahrheit gesagt habe
Über die Herrschenden, braucht der Totenvogel davon
Nicht erst in Kenntnis zu setzen. (9, 815f.)

These three poems are revealing in two respects. First, they provided Brecht with the opportunity for a most telling personal testimony—about the purity, indeed the "autarky," of art; secondly, they are filled—again—with extreme poetic splendor, and not *although*, but rather *because* they are so completely identical with their historical moment. Each one of these poems is a pure nature poem and at the same time a great political lyric, a timeless idyll and a historical epigram. They are filled to the brim with this double reality and all the concomitant contradictions, and yet they are also well-balanced.

And almost like a *leitmotif*, these contrasts are once again those between the peaceful world of trees and the pitiless, murderous world of persecutions and the ever-threatening war of annihilation; the contrast between the "talk" about the former, which will not be silenced, and the "silence" about the latter, which becomes an admonishing, warning, far-resounding voice. When "the distant thunder of naval gunfire" blends with the twittering of birds, those natural sounds of silence, lyrical mood and political statement are truly inseparable.

Should, after all, Brecht's purity and autarky of art consist of that? But as much as he was of one mind with Me-ti about such poems, he also agreed with Kin-jeh that this was a "Bad Time for Poetry." His like-named and highly lyrical confession also stems from those years "under the Danish thatched roof." And in it, too, are some of the most impressive and famous lines from Brecht's exile:

> Ich weiß doch: der Glückliche
> Ist beliebt. Seine Stimme
> Hört man gern. Sein Gesicht ist schön.
>
> Der verkrüppelte Baum im Hof
> Zeigt auf den schlechten Boden, aber
> Die Vorübergehenden schimpfen ihn einen Krüppel
> Doch mit Recht.
>
> Die grünen Boote und die lustigen Segel des Sundes
> Sehe ich nicht. Von allem
> Sehe ich nur der Fischer rissiges Garnnetz.
> Warum rede ich nur davon
> Daß die vierzigjährige Häuslerin gekrümmt geht?
> Die Brüste der Mädchen
> Sind warm wie ehedem.
>
> In meinem Lied ein Reim
> Käme mir fast vor wie Übermut.
>
> In mir streiten sich
> Die Begeisterung über den blühenden Apfelbaum
> Und das Entsetzen über die Reden des Anstreichers.
> Aber nur das zweite
> Drängt mich zum Schreibtisch. (9, 743f.)

Here, again, Kin-jeh's impressions of nature along with Brecht's sensations of the flesh are contrasted with the political and socio-historical moment, and thereby incorporated within poetry. Again we encounter that telling word "almost," wherein the voice of Me-ti, the advocate of art, speaks both cautiously and audibly. Quite consistently, the "rhyme," that is artistry, has taken the place of the simple "talk." To be sure, instead of the term "crime" there is now "insolence"—much more innocent, yet at the same time much more revealing. But for all that, Brecht's verses are no less serious and moving. It is no accident that the "dancing sails" are contrasted with the "torn nets," and the "stooped village woman," with the "young girls." All this corresponds exactly with the *leitmotif* of the trees which appears not solely in the image of a "blossoming apple tree" but is complemented by the opposite image of the "crippled tree in the yard." Such opposites are equally characteristic of Brecht—think of "Der Pflaumenbaum," likewise from his *Svendborger Gedichte,* or of the "Morgendliche Rede an den Baum Griehn" from his *Hauspostille.* But there is no need to go into that any more than it would be into his formal, purely technical innovations. Suffice it to say that the poet again makes use of the "evocation through negation," which banishes the naturally beautiful and humanly round into the realm of nothingness and thereby summons them into existence and permanence. For Brecht saw very well and celebrated those things which he claimed not to see or celebrate, such as "the green boats and the dancing sails on the Sound." The battle between poetic "enthusiasm" and political "loathing" (and not merely about the "speeches of the house painter" and the fascist scum) constantly raged in him. And although "only" the latter drove him "to his desk," he did write all the more grippingly about the former.

That this *poésie engagée* (to coin a new Sartrean term) is firmly anchored both in the historical as well as lyrical moment is also evidenced in poems from Brecht's Finnish and American exile. Even their titles are, for the most part, extremely concrete. Thus, for example, two strophes—which actually indulge in the luxury of rhyme—celebrate a "Finnische Gutsspeisekammer 1940." Brecht, who treasured the low as well as the high, who enjoyed the pleasures "of taste and testicles" (as his corpulent *Glücksgott* sings [10, 892]) as much as delights of a more subtle kind, transforms even a rural larder into a political poem:

> O schattige Speise! Einer dunklen Tanne
> Geruch geht nächtlich brausend in dich ein
> Und mischt sich mit dem süßer Milch aus großer Kanne
> Und dem des Räucherspecks vom kalten Stein.
>
> Bier, Ziegenkäse, frisches Brot und Beere
> Gepflückt im grauen Strauch, wenn Frühtau fällt!
> Oh könnt ich laden euch, die überm Meere
> Der Krieg der leeren Mägen hält! (9, 820)

Here, too, one could investigate formal details—the so-called "subtleties of expression," which Brecht supposedly ought to have avoided—and their artistic achievement. The opportunity would present itself especially in the phonetic area. But in the intellectual sphere, one could also go into the conceptions—so characteristic of Brecht—of fortune and the state of happiness which do not merely creep up around the central figure of the Chinese god of good fortune: they are of equal importance elsewhere in Brecht's *œuvre*. To every person who has a healthy sense and sensitivity, such "forbidden" artistic fruits are quite evident.

Therefore, let us take a look at a similar poem from the same time! In spite of its poetic title, "Finnische Landschaft," it, too, is very political:

> Fischreiche Wässer! Schönbaumige Wälder!
> Birken- und Beerenduft!
> Vieltöniger Wind, durchschaukelnd eine Luft
> So mild, als stünden jene eisernen Milchbehälter
> Die dort vom weißen Gute rollen, offen!
> Geruch und Ton und Bild und Sinn verschwimmt.
> Der Flüchtling sitzt im Erlengrund und nimmt
> Sein schwieriges Handwerk wieder auf: das Hoffen.
>
> Er achtet gut der schöngehäuften Ähre
> Und starker Kreatur, die sich zum Wasser neigt
> Doch derer auch, die Korn und Milch nicht nährt.
> Er fragt die Fähre, die mit Stämmen fährt:
> Ist dies das Holz, ohn das kein Holzbein wäre?
> Und sieht ein Volk, das in zwei Sprachen schweigt. (9, 822)

Brecht could not prevent nature, in all its beauty and majesty, from constantly intruding on him, indeed almost overpowering him. But did he want to prevent this at all? Almost hymnically the poet invokes the "waters" and "forests," the "mild air" and the earth with its "scents of berries and of birches"; it is almost a poem about the elements which he unfolds in these lines (something one of his heirs, Johannes Bobrowski, later did).[4] But not even here does the landscape become an end unto itself. To be sure, the poetic elevation takes place; and it is enchanting enough. But then the political "refugee," seemingly sitting so romantically beneath the trees, "turns again to his laborious job: continued hoping." It is a hoping and an unswerving laboring not only for the end of the war, but also for the end of all "disorder" and "exploitation," in the country as well as "in our cities of class struggle." All natural and sensual impressions, all those so intensively, so hymnically conjured moods and sensations grow pale, become blurred, and vanish. Brecht enumerates them carefully: "Dizzy with sight and sound and thought and smell." For precisely by not being permitted to remain in life, they are preserved in art, even if only to return someday more secure and more tangible, as the refugee and the poet earnestly hoped. But linked to them are the bitter reality and the present: "a people silent in two tongues." This unforgettable line, this eloquent "rhyme" about silence which closes the strophe, crowns the entire poem and rounds it off into a flawless work of art. It is—like each one of these confessions of a poet, these poetic-political dialogues and monologues "about trees"—anything but "insolent" or even "a crime."

Quite the contrary, this is the purest humane art striving for the purest humanity.

Perhaps now we understand what it meant for a poet like Brecht to write verses like the following:

> Aber auch ich auf dem letzten Boot
> Sah noch den Frohsinn des Frührots im Takelzeug
> Und der Delphine graulichte Leiber, tauchend
> Aus der Japanischen See.
> Und die Pferdewäglein mit dem Goldbeschlag
> Und die rosa Armschleier der Matronen
> In den Gassen des gezeichneten Manila
> Sah auch der Flüchtling mit Freude.
> Die Öltürme und dürstenden Gärten von Los Angeles
> Und die abendlichen Schluchten Kaliforniens und die Obstmärkte
> Ließen auch den Boten des Unglücks
> Nicht kalt. (10, 830)

Precisely these lines—although again rhymeless, irregular, and almost prose, again composed in "sparse speech," as the poet said of his play, *Die Mutter*—but precisely these poor twelve lines were "already too lavish,"too sumptuous for the refugee. Brecht jotted down this remark, literally, in his diary toward the end of 1944.[5] Even "The Landscape of Exile" (as this poem is entitled) was too lush for him: not *although*, but rather *because* he had stated directly—a quality which he otherwise found most praiseworthy— that which he claimed was no longer capable of direct expression. Brecht realized that he had esteemed things and their beauty not just highly, but too highly. For he neither eliminates them, in the sense of Mallarmé, through sheer negation, nor does he confront them with an aggressive affirmation in the sense of his own conception of art as a weapon. The poet of class struggle ventured one single time to speak lyrically without any restraint—something he had always desired, something, however, he could never give in to. This time he "saw"; indeed, he "beheld with joy." And what he saw, he celebrated. If this "refugee," the "messenger of misfortune," finally does negate, then this happens clearly with a reverse assessment. The "oil derricks" and the "thirsty gardens," the "ravines at evening" and the "fruit market" do not leave even him "*un*moved."

Bobrowski, too, that eager disciple of Brecht's, was driven to a celebratory, a laudatory appeal; he, too, longed for incessant naming ("Immer zu benennen," as the title of one of his most confessional poems reads):

> Immer zu benennen:
> den Baum, den Vogel im Flug,
> den rötlichen Fels, wo der Strom
> zieht, grün, und den Fisch
> im weißen Rauch, wenn es dunkelt
> über die Wälder herab.

But even Bobrowski, who abandoned himself to pure nature much more than did Brecht, was aware of the deceptiveness of poetic color and the enticement of lyrical symbols:

> Zeichen, Farben, es ist
> ein Spiel, ich bin bedenklich,
> es möchte nicht enden
> gerecht.[6]

For the sake of such justice Brecht rejected his own twelve gripping lines, which are among the most tender and moving (I am not afraid of that word) in his entire poetry. "Poems like 'The Landscape of Exile' will not be included," he wrote when putting together his collection of *Gedichte im Exil*, "they are simply too lavish."[7] Like Bobrowski, Brecht found the aesthetic "game" to be "dubious." Like Kin-jeh, he shrank back from that which it "implies"—even if only in retrospect. "Solely because of the increasing disorder" did this poet henceforth intend to speak and write—this poet who once cynically, in a Baal-like approval of the richly contradictory world with its "snowfalls" and its "lured flesh," had called himself the "poor B. B."!

But if, within the Brechtian confessions, this poem is exactly as striking as the lines with which we began, then one can hardly classify them as being too "lush." For their author intends to speak only "about the disorder," about "exploitation" and "class justice." Truly, we find in them the most extreme austerity of expression, barrenness and bareness alike, indeed absolute "privation," as Brecht acknowledged in his diary.[8] But from this very privation in "expression" as well as in "rhythm"—a blunt addition of the poet—the text gains its expressive power and rhythmic variety; from this alone derives its force, its almost unbearable plenitude and poetic intensity. If it is true that anything at all in Brecht's lyric is indeed written "in a kind of 'basic German' " (as he himself once asserted),[9] then these verses have to be cited. Yet they form a poem, which can profoundly move us even today, and perhaps nowadays more than ever.

But for what reason does Brecht no longer want to observe that which is aesthetic? Why does he no longer want to enjoy and create—either for himself or his fellow human beings—that which is human, round, and beautiful? Why does this poet now allow only for battle, "barrenness," and the "business of politics"—not for art and the unrestrained poetic variety of the world? "Solely" and exclusively

> Damit nicht dieses furchtbare gedrängte Zusammensein
> Von Schneefällen (sie sind nicht nur kalt, wir wissen's)
> Ausbeutung, verlocktem Fleisch und Klassenjustiz eine Billigung
> So vielseitiger Welt in uns erzeuge, Lust an
> Den Widersprüchen solch blutigen Lebens . . .

Brecht was artist enough not only to experience and realize the intense inhumanness of art (or the threat to all art from inhumanity) but also expressly to acknowledge it. That he dared to admit this to himself and to us is the ultimate, the truly shocking, confession of this poet.

Is, then, art *not* to be? The answer of Brecht the artist is that actually it shouldn't. *Art should not exist*—precisely because, in spite of its allure to him, it still seems to be a crime, something wanton, a blatant injustice, and barbaric; because man is still like a wolf to his fellow men; because today, as in times past, entire peoples and continents are being enslaved, exploited, and ground to dust; because this brutish "humanity" simply cannot go on lest it choke on its own bloody slime.

And yet, *art should exist.* Its inhumanity *and* its humanity are, for Brecht, both equally real and cannot be dismissed. The immorality, inhumanity, indeed *impossibility* of art exist side by side with the morality, humanity, indeed *necessity* of art; they even are incorporated and blended together. And only thus do they constitute the *reality of art.* Like the world, art is sorrowfully negated by Brecht and joyfully affirmed, rejected and yet accepted. It does exist: but its rending contradictions, its gaping contrasts remain with the poet. Were they reconciled in him, the man and artist and fighter Bertolt Brecht? Are they in his verses? Will they ever really be in the life of mankind, Brecht's faith notwithstanding?

This extraordinary poem ends with a gesture of utter simplicity, indeed almost of helplessness and despondency. "You understand?" O yes, poor and yet so rich Bertolt Brecht, we understand. At least we think we do.[10]

(Transl. from the German by Francis G. Gentry)

[1]From "Un coup de dés"; cf. Stéphane Mallarmé, *Sämtliche Gedichte.* Französisch mit deutscher Übertragung von Carl Fischer (Heidelberg: Schneider, 1957), p. 173.

[2]Hugo Friedrich, *Die Struktur der modernen Lyrik: Von Baudelaire bis zur Gegenwart* (Hamburg: Rowohlt, 1956), pp. 75, 81, 96.

[3]See Ernst Fischer, *Von der Notwendigkeit der Kunst* (Hamburg: Claassen, 1967).

[4]See "Versuch über Lyrik und Sprachbau," in my book *Strukturen: Essays zur deutschen Literatur* (Göttingen: Sachse & Pohl, 1963), p. 172ff.

[5]Bertolt Brecht, *Arbeitsjournal,* hrsg. von Werner Hecht (Frankfurt: Suhrkamp, 1973), II, 658.

[6]Johannes Bobrowski, *Schattenland. Ströme* (Stuttgart: Deutsche Verlags-Anstalt, [2]1962), p. 86.

[7]Brecht, *Arbeitsjournal,* II, 715.

[8]Ibid.

[9]Ibid.

[10]For the unabridged German version of this essay, see my collection, *Brecht und Nietzsche oder Geständnisse eines Dichters: Fünf Essays und ein Bruchstück* (Frankfurt: Suhrkamp, 1979), pp. 11ff.

"Grenzverschiebung":
Günter Kunert's Humanistic Stance

A. LESLIE WILLSON

The humanist in a technological world feels himself embattled. With humanistic values that he finds difficult to describe, he assumes a defensive posture and must pit abstractions—concepts and ideas—against the practical, shiny, life-enhancing instruments of the technologist. The encounter is not new—it seems to be an almost perennial struggle between the forces of technology and science and the adherents of usually ill-defined humanistic concerns. Solutions from the realms of philosophy, politics, and sociology have repeatedly resulted in stalemate—the on-going battle seems best managed in the hands of artists, and particularly in those of writers, who marshal their concern for humanity with the rich metaphorical and symbolic human attribute that is universal and unique: with language.

Four areas of humanistic concern occupy the attention of the humanist: 1) The dignity of man, man held to be a singular creature, a being obsessed with the necessity of making morally valid decisions, a being subject to the strains and ecstasies of emotions, a supremely individual being aware of the obliteration of his individuality in death. 2) Man's quest for social equity, for though an individual, he is also a social creature which for its own sake must seek justice for its fellows with a spirit of tolerance and a compassion for otherness, whether that otherness be sexual, ethnic, religious, or economic. 3) Man's prophetic vision of history, which involves his relationship with the state, his defense of individual liberty, his involvement with the brutalities of warfare, and very specifically his preoccupation with the past in terms of memory, and hence with the triadic structure of time: past, present, and future. 4) Man's incessant effort to communicate meaningfully and clearly with his fellow-man, his attempt to come to terms with the paradoxes inherent in the communicative modes, whether they be in the graphic arts, in music, or in literary forms.

Günter Kunert is an author who persistently sides with humankind against the forces arrayed against it. Though a Communist of long standing, a citizen of a socialist state even while living abroad, and politically an adherent of a socialist-focused ideology, Kunert is foremost a writer whose principal concern is humankind, not the socialist or democratic or political human being. A prolific and almost insatiable writer, Kunert has refused today to the ideology he espouses. His insistence on writing about those matters that threaten to overwhelm and obliterate humanity has brought him official reprimands from his own GDR government, but also has brought him to the attention of readers outside of the boundaries of his homeland, and brought him international recognition that promises to increase the more he is translated into other tongues. Kunert's path is not an easy one. In order to traverse a road guarded by censors he has employed the subtleties of irony, the delights of impish wit, and a constant irridescent intelligence. In novels, essays, stories, poems, and radio plays he returns again and again to his main concern: the welfare of the puny but lovable human animal.

As Ian Hilton mentions in an article entitled "Günter Kunert: The Way Ahead," published in the Winter 1976 issue of *Books Abroad*, Kunert has been attacked in East Germany for his "apathy to socialism and a nihilistic outlook." But throughout "Kunert has remained constant in his express concern for humanity."[1] Hilton points out that, with such a concern, "it is natural that Kunert should write poems referring to specific persons, for people provide the thread of historical perspective and embrace different aspects of human contact (and non-contact) and attitudes toward life. The fact that many of the figures introduced in the poems were (or are) writers indicates Kunert's preoccupation with the role of the individual as a human being and political animal as well as with that of the artist in society."[2] Like any writer, Kunert writes about people and places—and places include the world of nature as well as man-made habitations ranging from great cities to single rooms. But unlike most writers, he also seeks to understand the dimension of the essence of a writer: language itself.

Kunert is concerned with the first area of humanistic interest: the dignity of man. In the poem "Mängel," he states that the obvious is difficult to recognize:

> . . . Wir kennen das Glück
> ganz genau und haben es niemals kennengelernt.
> Wir könnten im Paradies leben
> hätten wir bloß
> keine feste Vorstellung davon. Menschen wären
> wir ohne Glauben an den Nutzen von Menschen.[3]

In these lines he pleads for a receptivity to what is obvious, and for the suspension of preconceptions. The value of mankind is an inherent quality that requires no definition, least of all that of utility. But given that man recognizes his worth, Kunert mourns in "Wunder erleiden" that human beings slaughter one another with great precision.[4] The poem "Selbstprüfung aus gegebenem Anlaß" reprimands man for not being more concerned with the welfare of his fellow-man, even though the poet realizes also that a human being finds sympathy difficult to express, that a human being guards his own self protectively from experiencing the fates of others.[5]

Conscious of his individual weakness and susceptibility to manipulation, the human being must resist those forces that reduce him to a mere social organism, something that he can accomplish only through scepticism, as Kunert states in the poem "Befragen heißt auch: in Frage stellen":

Befragen die Rauchsäule
nach ihrem bedrohlichen Ursprung

am Boden die Ameise nach ihrem Weg
und die kreisenden Satelliten
was für ein Bild sie sich von dir machen
ob etwa
wie von einer Ameise am Boden.[6]

Man is paradoxically and inextricably bound with other men; he cannot escape that existential fact, which is as much a part of him as is a sentence imposed on a lawbreaker, a thesis that Kunert states in the poem "Tage und Tage."[7]

It is ironic that man must work at being human, must make an effort to maintain his individuality. He must resist the weaknesses of his own nature and, even though it be with a mere cautionary and sceptical interjection, he must concern himself with all human beings. This is the message of Kunert's poem "Das kleine Aber." The irony that invests the poem emphasizes the paradox that man must be involved in what affects his fellow-man while still preserving his own individuality. Man is one and he is many, and what befalls many must involve each one singularly. Still, man must not sacrifice his unique self in the brackish wake of the mass of man. Kunert points out scathingly that the greatest crimes have occurred in the name of *all*. He does not disguise the fact that man fulfills his destiny only with difficulty and risk.[8]

Under the rubric of the second concern of the humanist, man's quest for social equity, can be placed the need for man to have a plan for himself. In the prose piece "Positives Glanzstück," Kunert admires with astonishment the order and utility of the cities man has built. A city map untucked from a breast pocket and spread out can guide any imaginative person through the maze of the most complicated city. Though history is rich with negative ideas, the city is a brilliant and positive human accomplishment. But now man must make a topographical map of his own self, locating those places where nature is impressive, where it has declined, where it has been destroyed, where it has disappeared. Such a map would point out the idiosyncrasies, mention the sewers, the wilderness areas, one-way streets of inhibited psyches, repeated tears, laughter on schedule, stations of hate and sympathy—all this would help man find himself. Kunert concludes that the only thing man lacks is the anciently sought reliable measure of himself.[9]

In the exemplary tale "Ich und ich," the narrator finds himself duplicated in a chance encounter. What puzzles him particularly is that his twin's gestures are synchronic with his own, a phenomenon that leads him to presume that the resemblance is not only physiognomical but psychological as well. Little by little, doubles appear: in the person of his postman, in a neighbor, even female doubles, and none seem to notice anything unusual. The narrator desperately searches for a non-double who might be able to explain what is occurring. In a tavern he finds one customer who does not look like him, but when he queries him a waitress in his facsimile appears promptly with the check and his non-double hurries out. The story concludes:

> Während er durch die Schwingtür verschwand, kam ein Trupp junger Selbste herein, die, da mein Tisch jetzt bis auf mich leer war, neben mir und mir gegenüber die Stühle hervorzogen und sich grußlos setzten. Sie ließen die Speisekarte herumwandern, redeten über Uhrzeit, Datum und Wetter, wobei sie so taten, als wüßten sie nicht ganz genau, daß es Mittwoch, der 19. November, zwölf Uhr fünfundvierzig sei und draußen gnadenloser Sonnenschein.[10]

The story is a parable of the horrors of conformity and the gruesome and regrettable loss of individuality. In it, the non-conformist is an outsider and eventually an outcast. Between the lines the reader is tempted to perceive a strong criticism of regimentation that molds men and women into impersonalities with indiscernible differences.

In the relationship between the sexes, Kunert emphasizes the capability of men and women to enter a communality of human endeavor. In his sketch "Eins plus eins gleich eins," he admits the difficulty a man has understanding a woman, since her physique is different, her psyche is different, her function in society is different, it having been shaped by what he calls "maskuline, glorreich-katastrophale Jahrtausende." The appointment of a woman to this committee or that council, in order to comply with the duty of tolerance, in reality simply emphasizes the exceptional character of such a procedure; it confirms the inferior status of woman through an amicable but brutal axiom. Kunert maintains that men and women share in common an understanding of what constitutes humanity and humane behavior.[11]

The intolerance manifested by the male toward the female in certain areas of social and behavior role-playing is echoed by another intolerance, that exhibited toward the Jew. In a poem entitled "H.H. postum ins Stammbuch," reminiscent in style and mood of Heinrich Heine, Kunert expresses his contempt for such prejudice.[12] Strong, playful, and at times even malicious irony is no stranger to Kunert's style. Furthermore, in the prose piece "Der verschlossene Raum," he endorses a Romantic trait that he himself manifests: riddles renew man's innate investigatory restlessness. Searches and paths to explore are unquenchably repeated. The character of man's life is that of being underway—it is not necessary that he reach his goal or find satisfaction in solving the riddles that confront him. Man's nature is to search ceaselessly and fruitlessly, and he is happiest in his search for essences. Fictions are the impulses of human longing.[13]

The third humanistic category involves man's memory of the past in the frame of history. The poem "Denkmal" is exemplary for the vacuous character of historical monuments that emphasizes man's transiency, a message of history that man usually overlooks.[14] In the poem "Tage und Tage," Kunert mentions that moments of historical stress produce the threat of honors, medals, and laurels, cause goodness to grow and humanity to overflow.[15] But the unnamed something that endures in the subconscious of certain generations of human beings is their only bequest, as Kunert says in the poem "Hinterlassenschaften." From historical evidence man knows that books burn well, and that human beings burn less well. History is the stepmother of mankind and furnishes him with dubious examples, golden words, final data that should guide him. Man has inherited axioms against which he can act, and experiences that he can deny. But for his part, writes Kunert, he will bequeath mankind his unmistakable fingerprint in a soap bubble.[16]

In a prose tribute to Oda Schrottmüller, a woman executed by the Nazis, Kunert remarks that the more heroes there are, the fewer human beings. Oda Schrottmüller was not a martyr, not a victim, not an object of suffering. In her effort to end suffering, with a pure heart to intercede in the impurity of criminal impulses, she demonstrated humanism in action.[17] Kunert's warning not to forget her is an expression of the importance he lends remembering, the exercise of memory. In the poem "Erinnern I," he lists destructive or inhibitory acts that are meant to bring forgetfulness, but result in its contrary:

> Die abgeschlagenen Köpfe
> der Statuen beweisen nicht
> das Vergessen. Gelöschte Inschriften
> sind unbesieglich. Auf dem Index
> der Päpste blüht Weltliteratur.
> Und die Flammen brennender Bücher
> beleuchten Jahrhunderte: unseren Weg
> aus dem Dunkel ins Dämmer.

The path of man from darkness into dawn is not without its dangers. The second strophe of the poem is an example of typical Kunert irony, a statement meant to reprimand the fickle and forgetful nature of man:

> Gedächtnisschwund begleitet
> das Schwinden der Armut, die
> ihren Aufenthalt wechselt, umzieht
> vom Magen zum Kopf:
> Es geht aufwärts!

But in the last strophe Kunert sees himself, the poet, as the preserver of memory:

Doch kein Erinnern stirbt ganz:
als Gespenst geht es um
in der Welt auf der Suche
nach Söhnen
und findet sie hier
und findet sie da
und findet mitten in meinem Zimmer
einen von ihnen für sich
zwischen Dämmer und Dunkel.[18]

Among the many roles Kunert assigns to the poet is the keeper and transmit-ter of memory in the time between dawn and darkness. In the poem "Rück-blick," Kunert states that man seems incapable of enjoying the present mo-ment but derives his satisfaction in retrospect, in the afterglow of transient happiness sinking behind the hills of memory.[19]

In the poem "Erinnern III," the past stirs indiscernibly in the move-ment of words. A shape in rude contours affirms a human being, though not whether man or woman. But a few buttons on an overcoat are firmly sewn on over a cross of black thread, and half-covered by the left lapel is glimpsed a yellow star—that is all.[20] With words Kunert adjures his reader to remem-ber. History is by definition something to be remembered, something past. But in the prose text "Exkursion in die Geschichte nebst Abschweifungen," Kunert criticizes the aptness of people to relegate history to the past. Most people, almost without exception, find the present unhistorical. Generally the feeling is that history begins only at a temporal remove of fifty or sixty years, as though—says Kunert—history were only that which is not person-ally connected, that which cannot be revived. Never was antiquity so ancient as today, he concludes with an ironic sparkle.[21] Human involvement in the past is not something easily forgotten or ignored—on the contrary, human beings must constantly be aware of the past and must be reminded of the commonplace that today's present is tomorrow's past.

As a poet, Kunert is particularly involved with the fourth area of hu-manistic endeavor, the area of communication between human beings. He is naturally particularly conscious of language and its quixotic and perishable nature. Language is a mixture of magic and surprise, of the literal and the figurative, as for example in the epigrammatic "Die Wirkung von Worten":

Die Wirkung von Worten

läßt sich schwer ermessen:
Guten Tag—das begreifst du noch,
aber daß der Tag trotzdem nicht
besser wird, setzt dich
in Erstaunen.[22]

A professional and adept manipulator of language, Kunert can afford to be critical, as he is in "Sprache II" where he suggests that nouns—the regents of language—have increased to such an extent that they threaten to suffocate in their own masses, or devour themselves through a lack of verbs, a class from which they raised themselves violently. Kunert believes that nouns should be transported back to their place of origin.[23]

Language is a fragile and insufficient vehicle for human expression. In "Sprache III," Kunert likens language to ships that follow a set course according to the measure of necessity, the law of the stars, and the weight of their freight. Sadly, though language has a firm destination, it is wrecked before it can reach port, for the prelinguistic thought becomes broader and weaker in the wake of language.[24] In "Sprache I," also entitled "Todesanzeige," Kunert mourns the increasing tendency of language to say and mean less and less. Philologists already are sticking a black flower into their lapels.[25] And what will happen when language perishes? "Und dann" recommends that human beings come to terms with one another through tender signs, raised hands, daggerless.[26]

Language and other modes of human communication are now, and have been, targets and victims of censorship, an act of vandalism and repression toward humanity that Kunert resists. In "Optik I," he says that the world is a book much too open and vulnerable to censors.[27] In his radio play "Ehrenhändel," the principal theme is resistance to censorship, there in the person of Heinrich Heine, the target of Prussian censors. Heine defiantly resists, as did Kunert. Since book-burners and censors consider the poet their enemy, the conscientious practitioner of poetry must ask himself, "Warum schreiben?" In the essay of that title, Kunert says that the writer writes because he thus journeys into an alien land where he can be himself, where he can discover the impersonal general constituents that are nevertheless, inherently, extremely private. Writing is a wavelike expansion in all directions, an expansion that ignores boundaries and absorbs and illuminates the unknown more and more. For Kunert writing is a ceaseless beginning, a repetitious first-time experience, like making love and experiencing pain. As long as the writer writes, he neither falls into ruin nor perishes. Kunert concludes by saying that he writes in order to endure a world that incessantly crumbles into nothingness.[28]

Though the writer expresses his essential humanity through the act of writing, his conscience gnaws at him occasionally in a world where utility is at a premium. Kunert solves this humanistic dilemma in defining the consciousness of a poem, in the essay "Bewußtsein des Gedichts." What he means by that term is the relatively autonomous process of intuitive knowledge on the basis of subjective empiricism, reflected in a specific form—the poem—and containing an unmistakable character. The consciousness of a poem is inextricably bound with the poem and with the poet, who may possess or even use other forms of consciousness, such as those from philosophy, politics, or economics that, however, need not coincide with the consciousness of the poem. It should be no surprise, the East German Kunert writes, that in poems a poet can depict aesthetic or political viewpoints that diverge from those he otherwise holds. If the consciousness of a poem were primarily the socially predominant consciousness of an epoch, then it would be completely determined by that epoch and would perish with the epoch's demise. Kunert concludes his remarks with frequently quoted words:

> Brauchen die Hungernden Gedichte? Sie brauchen Nahrung, soviel ist sicher. Aber sie brauchen genauso das Bewußtsein ihres ihnen vorenthaltenen Menschentums und damit die Gewißheit, daß ihnen mehr fehlt als die Befriedigung ihrer Bedürfnisse, gleichgültig wie immer die Bedürfnisse steigen werden, und wie deren Befriedigung.[29]

It is obvious that a poem occupies a paradoxical position in a world in which serviceability and maximal utility are lauded. The poem serves no practical end, neither that of entertainment nor of information nor even of recreation. The purpose of a poem is much more discreet and cryptic, less comprehensible, not measurable on common scales of comparison. In Kunert's opinion, the purpose of a poem, as he states in the essay "Paradoxie als Prinzip," involves the reader, who in coming to terms with a poem must also come to terms with himself. In reading a poem, the reader becomes paradoxically identical and at the same time not identical with the poet. The poem colors the psyche of the reader and he casts his reflection onto the poem. Kunert surmises that the act of reading a poem results in a reduction of the coarseness of the reader, that it is a process of sublimation, of an enhancement of his humanity.[30]

In a debate on the question "For whom does a writer write?" that broke into the pages of *Sinn und Form* in 1972, Kunert maintains that the act of writing is one of self-liberation, of self-understanding, of self-realization, the only possible act of individualization, of the discovery of one's own identity. And if that process is successful for the poet, then the reader of the poem shares in the poet's experience. Thus, says Kunert, neither at the beginning nor at the conclusion of the act of composition does the poet ask himself "For whom?" He continues specifically:

> Die Vorstellung von einem sozial oder ideologisch begrenzten Publikum (das im Ernst gar nicht existiert) führt zur bekannten Konsequenz der Selbstbeschreibung, zu einer Reduktionskunst, die selbst jene nicht erreicht, die sie eigentlich erreichen will. Sie vergaß nämlich über dem sozialen, politischen, ideologischen, nationalen, ökonomischen Status ihres Publikums, daß dessen Status primär ein menschlicher ist: kein rousseauisch-naturhafter, wohl aber ein über Epochen hinweg entstandener zivilisatorischer, dem das Soziale, Politische, Ideologische als instabiles Agens beigeordnet ist. Und daß außerdem Kunst, Literatur, Lyrik, welche Bezeichnung man auch wählen mag, Grenz-

überschreitung bedeutet: eine Literatur für streng presbyterianische
Handwerksgesellen von Orten unter 30 000 Einwohnern über das presbyterianische Handwerksgesellenproblem ist keine.[31]

This statement, more than any other, emphasizes Kunert's dedication to humanistic ideals. Social, political, and ideological matters are considered unstable and thus are relegated to a subsidiary status in human affairs. By its
very definition the action of an artist with humanistic aspirations breaks
through boundaries, pushes them back, crosses over them. In his poem
"Beichte," Kunert sums up the emotion the artist feels:

Beim Übertritt
an allen Grenzen zwischen hier und dort
zwischen Oberlippe und Unterlippe
zwischen Wahrheit und Sicherheit
schlägt uns jedesmal das Herz viel zu schnell.[32]

Those lines summarize not only the experience of the humanistic poet, Günter Kunert, but also the experience of any human being who crosses boundaries in a strange, new world.

When Kunert crossed boundaries between Buch on the northeast outskirts of East Berlin to Itzehoe near Hamburg in the early fall of 1979, he
found his voice again after months of solitary depression and bereavement at
the coming loss of his home. It was an angry and more outspoken voice that
was heard in his monologue, "Jetzt ist es endgültig genug!" published on 9
November 1979 in *Die Zeit*, but written the previous May. In the article, he
apologizes for speaking on his own behalf and then proceeds to castigate the
East German bureaucrats, party hacks, and slavish professorial and critical
adherents of a system that finally succeeded in driving him away from his
homeland. He does not mince words. He speaks of the intellectual attitude
of persons who judged literature for thirty years with misjudgments unrelated to facts. He mentions Renate Drenkow and accuses her of threatening
him through her statement about how tedious it was to read Kunert, and
who complained about his historical pessimism. She accused him of thus
damaging the literature of the GDR, but he wonders whether her accusation
is not more damaging than the twenty-three books he had published,
whether the regimentation, the exploitation, and public banishment were
not more destructive. Further she mentioned Kunert in a manner that separated his own works from that of GDR literature.

Kunert, in the same article, accuses Hans Koch of being a manipulator
of truth because Koch misused a Kunert poem, "Gesang für die im Zwielicht
lebten" from *Tagwerke* (1961, but written between 1953 and 1957), in con-
trasting it with Christa Wolf's novel *Der geteilte Himmel*: first of all because
Koch misread (whether deliberately or not) the title and cited it as "Gesang
für die im Zwielicht leben" instead of "lebten." When Kunert wrote his state-

ment of protest in May of 1979, he ended with a declaration that the aban-
donment of a literary role in GDR literature was not the only alternative—
there must be others. But when the article was published in November, he
too had left his home and his heritage behind.

The renewed voice of Kunert in the West laments with nostalgia mixed
with relief and some bit of ironic alienation, as is apparent in the first poems
published in *Die Zeit* on 11 January 1980, one of which summarizes the
mixed feeling of frustration and ease that he felt while unpacking in Itzehoe.
The poem is entitled "Platzwechsel":

> Schmutzig ist der Stoff
> an den Knien: Noch immer trage ich
> die Hose so wie ich herkam
> Tage gleich Jahreszeit
> morgens Sonne mittags Hagel
> gehen geschäftig draußen vorüber
> indes ich nur
> einen Schrank rücke Vorhänge befestige
> Kisten öffne in denen mir
> die Vergangenheit folgte
> bruchsicher verpackt:
> Nicht eine Erinnerung
> wurde beschädigt
> aber keine will mir mehr gehören

The voice of Kunert is heard most clearly and again steadfastly in the
book of poems published in the fall of 1980 by the Hanser Verlag under the
title *Abtötungsverfahren*, a title that is both accusatory and descriptive.
Kunert speaks plainly and calmly, looking back with new awareness in the
poem "Rückblick," which had appeared previously in *Die Zeit* of 11 January
1980:

> Dem eigenen fremden Leib
> entschlüpft
> ledig der Last
> und aus der Ferne
> einen verdorrten Leichnam
> einen Kokon
> seh ich an meinerstatt
>
> Ein gewisser Tod
> hatte sich bei mir angemeldet
> erster Vorsitzender der guten
> oder sogar besten Gesellschaft
> aller denkbaren doch
> ich entkam ihm
> nordwärts in ein neues Hemd

und in Richtung
Ultima ratio[34]

Officially, Kunert left the GDR with an exit visa valid for 1050 days—
three years. He insisted at first that his move was of a temporary nature, and
he obviously would like to think of East Berlin as his former and future
home.[35] But the ironic voice and its bitter air of finality almost preclude such
a return, however longed for, as is evident in the last stanza of the poem
"Berlin":

jetzt ist alles benannt und vermessen
abgeheftet und niedergerissen
und nichts mehr da
zum Beschreiben.[36]

The kind of officially sanctioned and programmed persecution and
pressure that eventually brought about Kunert's departure from the GDR is
described in the poem "Belagerungszustand":

Sie kommen direkt aus dem Hauptquartier
der Utopie in Berlin-Lichtenberg
rauchen und lesen Zeitung und
erwarten den Widersatz
meiner armen und zaghaften Worte
frisch geschlüpfte Zugvögel
Wegbereiter
dorthin wo das Gespräch über Bäume
kein Schweigen mehr bindet
dorthin wo keiner einem
die Sprache verschlägt[37]

Finally, in the alien but protective mists of North Germany, Kunert
comes to an insight after his persistent but vain attempts to make forbidden
statements "am Rande" in the midst of his humanistically inimical oppo-
nents in the German Democratic Republic. In the poem "Einsicht," he says:

Unter den spät gekeimten Einsichten
auch meine
Unter den ausgebeutelten Seelen
auch ich
Sanft verstoßen: Das gebe ich zu
aus längst wuchernder Fremde

Ich saß am Tisch und wußte nicht
wer
und am Fenster dasselbe und so
Tag wie Nacht

Jedes Wort griff mich an
und forderte meinen Kopf

mein Nicken oder genügsam
bloß mein Verstummen: Das gebe ich zu
damit es selber nur sei

Vermutlich wurden meine Stunden gezählt
meine Briefe mein Geld mein Verbrechen
die gebe ich zu:
Wiederholtes Schweigen

Vermutlich wurde lange
mit mir gerechnet aber es kam
nichts dabei heraus
Weg damit
Wenigstens sanft
immerhin[38]

The humanist Günter Kunert, struck dumb with frustration and indignation after the expulsion of Wolf Biermann from East Germany in November 1976, ended his repeated silences and again took up his pen in defense of humanity, the humane, the freedom of expression, even though his voice occasionally prophesies disappointment and doom. Kunert admonishes and cautions and remains pessimistic, but he also retains his deep belief in the essential good and right of human beings. His utterances are made in the unmistakable voice of humanity. And he still sends his friends New Year's greetings.

[1]Ian Hilton, "Günter Kunert: The Way Ahead," *Books Abroad*, 50 (1976), p. 46.
[2]Hilton, p. 52.
[3]Günter Kunert, *Im weiteren Fortgang* (Munich: Hanser, 1974), p. 64.
[4]Ibid., p. 21.
[5]Günter Kunert, *Das kleine Aber* (Berlin: Aufbau-Verlag, 1975), pp. 67f.
[6]*Fortgang*, p. 19.
[7]Ibid., p. 12.
[8]*Aber*, p. 11.
[9]Günter Kunert, *Die geheime Bibliothek* (Berlin: Aufbau-Verlag, 1973), pp. 105f.
[10]Ibid., p. 48.
[11]Ibid., pp. 137ff.
[12]*Aber*, p. 91.
[13]*Bibliothek*, pp. 9f.
[14]*Fortgang*, p. 71.
[15]Ibid., p. 12.
[16]*Aber*, p. 72.
[17]*Bibliothek*, pp. 218f.
[18]*Fortgang*, p. 14.
[19]Ibid., p. 93.
[20]Ibid., p. 94.
[21]Günter Kunert, *Tagträume in Berlin und andernorts* (Munich: Hanser, 1972), p. 156.
[22]*Fortgang*, p. 35.
[23]Ibid., p. 28.
[24]Ibid., p. 29.

[25]*Aber*, p. 26.

[26]Ibid., p. 27.

[27]*Fortgang*, p. 60.

[28]*Tagträume*, p. 326.

[29]Ibid., p. 322.

[30]*Bibliothek*, p. 275.

[31]Günter Kunert, "Literatur als Grenzüberschreitung," *Tintenfisch* 7 (Berlin: Klaus Wagenbach, 1974), p. 61.

[32]*Aber*, p. 7.

[33]It is the first poem in the collection *Abtötungsverfahren* (Munich: Hanser, 1980), p. 7, where it has been slightly revised.

[34]"Rückblick" is the second poem in *Abtötungsverfahren*, p. 8.

[35]*Abtötungsverfahren* is dedicated to Kunert's wife: "Für M.—einer Mitbürgerin zwischen den Stühlen."

[36]*Abtötungsverfahren*, p. 43.

[37]Ibid., p. 50.

[38]Ibid., p. 91.

What Is Austrian Literature?
The Example of H.C. Artmann
and Helmut Qualtinger

Egon Schwarz

Even though the problem expressed in the title has occupied me in one fashion or another throughout my conscious life, I have come to the conclusion that it is too complex to admit of an absolutely satisfying solution. It goes to the heart of cultural history and entails an understanding of the highly delicate relationship between the products of the human mind and the society in which they are embedded. Nevertheless I hold the reflections here involved to be legitimate and profound ones, well worth continued exploration. Although the answers, at the present state of understanding, will necessarily remain partial and inadequate, there are other and less appropriate procedures, or, in my opinion, even totally unacceptable ones, that have been adopted in tackling our puzzle. This alone justifies, it seems to me, every effort, no matter how inconclusive the result.

One thing becomes clear very early in the investigation: that in reality one is not dealing with a single question at all, but with a whole cluster of related queries. It is not merely a matter of asking: *What* is Austrian literature? We have to ask more fundamentally: *Is* there an Austrian literature? In what *sense* can there be an Austrian literature? Or more precisely: In what ways is it *fruitful* to speak of an Austrian literature? And last not least: What do we *gain* or *learn* by postulating the existence of an Austrian literature? Hardly have we formulated these questions when we realize that one cannot hope to answer them one by one, but that they are interrelated, each influencing and determining the other, so that we have to keep them all present in our minds.

Let me give an illustration. An empirically minded person might suggest that we simplify matters considerably by calling Austrian the literature produced by holders of Austrian passports or, less facetiously, by writers born and raised in Austria, no matter what the size and shape of the country may have been at the time. This would provide us with a pragmatic definition of the terms and allow us to proceed, unencumbered by esoteric and useless intellectual exercises, toward the reading and understanding of a given poetic work. Such a procedure is followed by many who deal with Austrian literature, particularly in classroom situations. There is nothing wrong with it and I recommend it heartily. But it does not answer our basic question, it does not even attempt to answer it, it simply does away with it. And it can do so because it completely ignores another question we have also encountered: What do we actually *gain* by speaking of an Austrian literature? If we follow that procedure we gain nothing and learn nothing, and it is pretty meaningless to raise the question in the first place.

But the problem won't go away, for two reasons. First, because of the self-understanding of many writers who consider themselves Austrian and take this to be an important part of their identity. Whether they are right or wrong in so thinking, such a self-definition on the part of a poet, novelist, or dramatist may have serious consequences for his entire orientation in life, and hence for his literary practice. The second reason applies to all of us as scholars. Many of the authors who wrote in the German language are, as we know, Austrian. It cannot be long before we discover the vast secondary literature that makes a great deal of the Austrianness of a given work or writer, and indeed of entire literary groups and periods, thereby raising, explicitly or inadvertently, some of the questions we have posed. The irksome feature in this practice is, however, that many take the answers for granted or proffer their explanations in a distorted or otherwise obnoxious manner which must not be left unchallenged.

By far the most common of these dubious shortcuts is the notion of national character. Those using this approach build their airy edifices on several presuppositions each of which is questionable in its own way: that the inhabitants of a country have in common a well-defined national character; that the literature of such a nation accurately reflects this national character; and that by analyzing literary works it is possible to recognize and describe it. Seldom is there to be found a consciousness of the intellectual and logical fragility of such undertakings. By what miraculous magic a complex and heterogeneous institution like literature is supposed to embody an ethereal substance such as the character of a nation is not perceived as a problem at all by these scholars, but accepted as a God-given fact. Moreover, their exercises in divination commonly suffer from another fundamental shortcoming, usually referred to as circular reasoning. Since other reliable sources are difficult to come by, they have an annoying habit of deducing the national character from the literature to which—*mirabile dictu*—they then retrace it, thus making national literature and national character into practically synonymous concepts.

The treatment of national character in these writings is in itself noteworthy. Rarely do their authors express an awareness that they are dealing with historically variable attitudes and patterns of behavior, or betray the insight that, for example, the belligerent Swedes of the Thirty Years' War seem to have had another "national essence" than the modern architects of the Swedish welfare state. They fail to realize that social groups in the same country develop different psychological modes of reaction, the result being that, let us say, Italian industrial workers seem to be more closely related to members of their own class in France than to the aristocracy in their own society, and vice versa; that agrarian nations differ from industrial ones not so much on the basis of national character as on that of their entire economic system; and that the industrial countries in turn evolve common qualities, compared to which national peculiarities are of minimal importance. Anyone even remotely inclined to deal with these questions must consider the possibility that regional differences are apt to counteract national uniformities: thus, to take an example from Germany, it may be difficult to discover the common German characteristics among the Westphalian and Bavarian peasant populations. Such regionalisms are peculiarly strong in a nation that had been divided into hundreds of independent and semi-independent knightly estates, imperial cities, bishoprics, counties, duchies, kingdoms, *etc.* until about a hundred years ago, and was only imperfectly united then. In spite of these marked regional differences, it would be nonsensical to speak of a typically Pomeranian or Holsteinian literature. Furthermore, we must keep in mind that large cities produce a culture different from that of small towns and the countryside; and that no single individual, let alone a highly idiosyncratic writer and artist, corresponds to such general categories. The randomly chosen Frenchman is by no means more light-hearted, elegant, or rational than his German counterpart, and the individual German is no more stolid, disciplined, humorless, profound, or whatever he is supposed to be, than a Frenchman. These alleged differences have in effect ceased to be of public significance, since it is in nobody's interest any more to harp on them; for we must also bear in mind that such observations can be, and often have been, parts of ideologies mobilized into political weapons by vested interests. Similarly and finally, we should not forget that all that subtle and intuitive speculation about national characteristics in people and literature has become extremely suspect, and that such a mode of thinking itself represents a phenomenon which can be isolated and categorized in historical terms. Its roots lie in the 17th and 18th centuries, the era of absolutism and the upwardly mobile middle class; it then experienced a tremendous spurt of growth in the second half of the 19th and the first third of the 20th centuries, due to the expansion of imperialism and chauvinism, various forms of irredentism, the ideas of social Darwinism, and the belief in blood and soil. And though it found its most horrifying expression in the insane exaggerations of fascism, it lingered on into the postwar era when it was still used for ideological purposes.[1]

All this is true of Austria as well, where the debate about fascism was strongly hampered by the untenable myth that she was a victim of this calamity rather than one of its promoters. The reluctance to "come to grips with the past," as the phrase goes, coupled with a compelling need for national

identity, is perhaps accountable for the fact that the disease which I am inclined to dub "Nadleritis"[2] produced its morbid symptoms well into the
1950's and 1960's. It is not out of malice, but rather from a sense of scholarly
obligation to document my case, as well as the desire to warn as concretely as
possible against dangers inherent in it, that I am going to cite a few examples. Not so long ago there appeared a little book in which this wishful Austrian thinking made its appearance once more.[3] One of the contributors felt
that "a desire for distance and a disbelief in efficacy" were typical traits of
the Austrian character as well as of Austrian literature. Particularly ludi-
crous was his claim that it is Austrian "to renounce all speculation," for if
there is anything speculative on earth it is this kind of generalization which
then, by its own definition, would be un-Austrian and defeats its own purpose. But I wish to stress that such pastime speculations are not restricted to
born Austrians, that quite a few would-be and elective Austrians are also
engaged in them—persons who, like many converts, can be more zealous
than the most militant natives.

Here are a few more traits that are typical for Austria. Austrians, we
are told, are sceptical of modernity, averse to anything great, anything loud
and violent; they distrust what others deem right and important, and yet
their thinking is radical, their feelings are hard, their pride is imperturbable
and metaphysical; but all of these tough properties are enveloped in a puffy
softness.[4] For another contributor, modesty and wisdom are the chief characteristics of Austrian writers.[5] No attempt is made to prove these conten-
tions, to offer any documentation for them, or to justify them by any of the
customary means of establishing truth.

I shall now cite a third author whose essay culminates in a eulogy of the
Austrian idiom, the very medium of Austrian literature. He doesn't analyze
it linguistically; rather, he evokes its "essence" by lighting metaphorical fire-
works. To emphasize its peculiar character he dubs the Austrian language
"das Austriakische," a term for which there is no convincing English equivalent. In this language one can hear vibrate, he claims, its Latin-Romance
heritage and feel the Celtic radiance in its veins, it forms a ringing mosaic
which jells into homogeneous sound patterns only at a proper distance.[6]

The examples could be multiplied almost at will, since the literature of
Austrian characterology is extensive. Another collection which I consulted
tenders its mystifications in a similar manner. Here, too, the obligatory cry
"What is Austrian," is voiced, not at all as a cry of despair or a question that
could be answered, but as a battle cry—for the farther the speculators remove themselves from the empirical and historical sphere, the more secure
they feel in the possession of an inalterable truth. Let me refer to an article
which announces, in its very title, a program that effectively excludes true
questioning: "Austria is a Form of Poetry" (*Dichtung*).[7] I shall quote from

this treatise extensively enough to arrange the material according to certain categories. These rubrics are:

Timelessness of Austrian literature:

Darin liegt vielleicht das Auszeichnendste und Einzigartige des Österreichertums, daß es nicht politisch oder national zum Selbstbewußtsein gelangte, vielmehr zuerst und zuletzt im Geistigen sich erkennt und benennt; über alle furchtbaren Entscheidungen hinweg, ungeachtet aller Verluste und Neuordnungen, bewahrte es sich die Geistesverfassung, die ein halbes Jahrtausend besiegelte.

Ahistoricity and incarnation in literature:

Während die politischen Umgestaltungen historisch geworden sind, ist das Geistige gegenwärtig geblieben; wenn Österreich sich in seinem größten repräsentativen Dichter, Franz Grillparzer, erkennt, vereinigt sich in seiner zeitlichen Erscheinung zugleich das Zeitlose, im Formlosen seines äußeren Lebensganges, der fast das ganze 19. Jahrhundert ausfüllte, das Wesen, welches sich in jeder Dramenszene, in jedem Epigramm, in jeder Aufzeichnung ausspricht. Hier gewinnt die österreichische Wesensart ihr selbstverständliches Gepräge . . .

Identification of the "national spirit" with literature:

In der Dichtung hat sich das Österreichische als Form unverwechselbar konstituiert, grenzenlose, universale Gehalte gültig und unzerstörbar gefaßt, geprägte Form, die sich im *Bruderzwist in Habsburg* oder im *Nachsommer* ebenso einsichtig kundgibt wie im *Rosenkavalier* oder dem *Schwierigen*.

Obliteration of psychological and social differences, especially class conflict:

In dieser Form erhebt sich das Menschliche zu jener Höhe, in welcher die Scheidungen von Tun and Leiden aufgehoben sind, wie diejenigen von Herrschaft und Dienst . . .

Of course, this does not remove from the Austrian experience, as the author significantly says in another place, the "Erbwissen um die echte Ständeordnung."

Needless to say that any translation of these nebulous visions would pose considerable problems. Invariably they would come out less blurred since the English language is lacking traditions of comparable fuzziness. Let me finally quote a passage without precise meaning, just to show the language of essences it employs, a language not altogether dissimilar to what Adorno called the "Jargon der Eigentlichkeit":

Kein titanisches oder prometheisches Aufbegehren sprengt das strenge und schlichte Maß, vielmehr gehorcht ihm alles Wirkliche. Form wird hier niemals als Wagnis verstanden, Dichtung als Alexanderzug bis an die Grenzen des Chaos und darüber hinaus, sie ist getreues Bewahren, wahrhaftes Bewältigen. Das Vage und Ungefähre hält sie ebenso von sich fern wie das Eruptive und

Entgrenzende. Nicht der großartigere Vorwurf, der grandiose Versuch verleiht der österreichischen Dichtung häufig den höheren Rang vor verwandten Werken, sondern das Formvollendete, die Präsenz des Vielfältigen, der Sinn für die Möglichkeiten, das Vermeiden alles Forcierten; dadurch gewinnen die Gemüts- und Seelenbewegungen ihre Wahrhaftigkeit; nicht zufällig erweisen sich die österreichischen Dichter darin als die legitimsten Goethe-Erben. Dabei darf man das Unaufdringliche und Einfache keineswegs mit dem Schalen verwechseln, das Herzlich-Warme mit dem Hausbackenen, das Maßvolle mit dem Trivialen.[8]

These passages must suffice. It would be easy to string together more such quotations *ad nauseam*, and it would not be difficult either to show that in spite of its vagueness, its pretense of aloofness from the struggles of the day, this gobbledygook is actually a typical expression of the restoration that took place in the 1950's. The peculiar thing is that Austria of all nations must be regarded as a most unlikely repository of eternal essences. To assume the existence of a single definable extract called "Austrian spirit," and pervading all poetic works from the *Nibelungenlied* to those of Ernst Jandl, as these propagandists obviously do, is absurd. Let me cite weighty doubts advanced by another observer, also a "professional Austrian," who perceives the uniqueness of Austria precisely in terms of indefinable multiplicity, but does so with a lot more circumspection.[9]

"Eigentlich hat es ein einigermaßen konstantes Faktum namens Österreich vor dem Ende des ersten Weltkriegs nicht gegeben," he insists. And his further remarks show how revealing even the slightest reference to a historical event, such as the First World War, can be. I shall quote his warnings at some length because there cannot be a more believable spokesman for the necessary caution *vis-à-vis* an irrational and intuitive approach to national essences than a writer who has penned entire books about the ethnopsychology of the Swiss and the Austrians:

Der Staat, an dessen Spitze der Kaiser von Österreich als König von Ungarn, Böhmen, Jerusalem usw. und Großherzog von Toscana stand, schloß zwar Ungarn und Böhmen, nicht aber Jerusalem und Toscana ein. Er hieß nicht etwa "Österreich," sondern vereinigte zwei Hälften, wobei die ungarische Hälfte außer dem Königreich Ungarn auch aus anderen, beispielsweise kroatischen Gebieten bestand, aber zumindest eindeutig "Ungarn" hieß, während die österreichische Hälfte der österreichisch-ungarischen Zweieinigkeit offiziell nicht etwa den Namen "Österreich" führte, sondern sich die im Reichsrat vertretenen Königreiche und Länder nannte und erst durch ein kaiserliches Handschreiben vom 10. Oktober 1915—drei Jahre vor Torschluß—offiziell den Namen "Kaisertum" Österreich erhielt (welch lohengrinische Namensnennung!).

He continues in this vein for quite a while, sounding again and again the refrain, "Wo bleibt bei alldem Österreich?" His answer:

Überall und nirgends. Die Schwierigkeiten der genauen Begriffsbestimmung werden schon aus diesen Andeutungen sehr deutlich, fast einzigartig. Es gibt Staaten, über deren Identität mit sich selbst kein Zweifel bestehen kann, wie immer ihr aktuelles politisches Geschick sich gestalten mag: Italien, Spanien, Griechenland, Schweden, Persien, China, Japan. Andere beziehen ihren allgemein gebräuchlichen Namen von einem Kern, einem Zentrum: wir sagen "Rußland" und meinen ein Gebilde, das unter anderem auch aus Rußland besteht, wir sagen "England" und meinen England, Schottland und Wales, dazu womöglich auch Irland und vielleicht sogar das gesamte Commonwealth, wir nennen den Teil und meinen das Ganze. Wir sagen anderseits "Amerika," nennen das Ganze und meinen nur einen Teil Nordamerikas. Was immer wir aber sagen, wir wissen genau, was gemeint ist. Sagen wir jedoch "Österreich," wissen wir selbst nicht genau, ob wir die neun Bundesländer von heute meinen oder das 1918 auseinandergefallene System der Königreiche und Länder. Und auch wenn wir das scheinbar so eindeutige Adjektiv "deutsch" aussprechen, ist es von Mißverständnissen belastet. Die "Deutschen in Österreich" waren nämlich im Habsburgerreich nicht etwa die Preußen, Sachsen, Schwaben oder Bayern, also deutsche Untertanen, welche sich in Österreich befanden, sondern die deutschsprechenden Untertanen Franz Josephs in Tirol, Vorarlberg, Steiermark, Kärnten, Salzburg, Ober- und Niederösterreich sowie Böhmen, Mähren, Schlesien, Krain, der Bukowina und anderen Kronländern. Es konnte sein, daß ein Prager, Brünner, Innsbrucker oder Grazer auf "die Deutschen" (in Bayern, Schwaben, Sachsen oder Preußen) schimpfte und seinerseits von seinen böhmischen, mährischen oder schlesischen Mit-"Österreichern" in tschechischer Sprache als "Deutscher" beschimpft wurde.

Are these the certainties upon which the edifice of a uniform Austrian literature is to be built, constant in time and space?

After this preparation it cannot come as a surprise if I confess to a certain scepticism toward universal solutions of humanistic problems. I do not believe in an Austrian literature as the unchangeable expression of a disembodied Austrian "spirit" that leaves all political, social, and economic matters behind, deeply buried, to use Schiller's phrase, in the dust of commonplace. Such a view is, in my opinion, itself political in a rather obvious way. The Danubian monarchy was much too fragmented into ethnic, linguistic, and geographic subdivisions, held together by mainly dynastic interests, to have produced a single unified literature that could be regarded as theirs by the Czechs and Germans, Croatians and Italians, the Poles, Jews, Slovaks, and Hungarians cohabiting in this empire. The First Republic, a rump state, truncated remnant of a more splendid past, lasted less than twenty years. It was too bewildered, too impoverished, too unaccustomed to itself, and too much lacking in identity to have produced a cohesive body of literature. The Second Republic has now been in existence a similar number of years. It is more homogeneous than its predecessor, surer of itself, and more prosperous. It is possible that in the course of time it will create conditions for an

Austrian literature truly representative of its culture. It is altogether possible that there already exist literary works expressive of the peculiarly Austrian post-war conditions. The question of national literature is an extremely tricky one, and it is not at all certain that there is such a thing as a *German* literature, disrupted as the history of that country has been. The experts speak of the beginnings of such a literature toward the end of the Wilhelminian Empire and during the Weimar Republic. In contrast, everybody believes in a coherent French literature, expression of a country that has enjoyed a long political and cultural continuity, a centralized administration, a great capital, a long tradition of respect for letters, a habit on the part of its literary practitioners to be concerned with more than their craft and to take an active interest in the life of the nation as a whole.

Still, I do not think the search for an Austrian literature is hopeless if one cautiously adopts a history-oriented approach. On the following pages, I shall reflect on this possibility, but am painfully aware that what I can present here will at best be *prolegomena* to the real thing. I believe it is possible to say a work of literature is Austrian if it demonstrably issues from Austrian social history, or can convincingly be shown to have a bearing on it. In order to make this definition fruitful it is of course necessary to abandon the fiction of national, racial, or ethnic essences, capable of surviving all vicissitudes of history and remaining the same once and for all. Instead of postulating the classlessness of literature, the historical approach will pay particular attention to the dynamic social conflicts, and, in general, proceed from the assumption that literary works are connected with the needs and desires of the social groups to which they are addressed.

By way of analogy, I should like to glance for an instant at the German Democratic Republic. There are excellent reasons to regard the literature of that country as possessing some cohesion because of its inevitable connection with the state. This relationship is of course eminently political and historical in that we can indicate with accuracy when GDR literature originated. But to be able to pinpoint the place a certain work occupies in the cultural fabric of the state, one has to study its fluctuating history rather carefully. No amount of divination and speculation about the East German national character will do any good. All of this, however, won't prevent the literary historian from examining the connections of this literature with its past models and its relationship to West Germany. On the contrary, I suspect that a great deal can be learned from the individual GDR writer's attitude toward the "cultural heritage" and toward the Federal Republic of Germany.

Similarly, the scholar who is interested in the literature of Austria will want to conduct his research in close collaboration with the historian, especially the social and psycho-historian. In order to grasp what may be peculiarly Austrian in a given period, he will have to be familiar with the concrete conditions prevailing at the time. To this extent the old hermeneutical pre-scription holds true: namely, each work will dictate the method by which it can best be understood. Or perhaps one should say that the work determines the *factors* rather than the *method* necessary for its interpretation.

Every historian worth his salt knows that history is generated by the subtle interplay of continuities and discontinuities. Among the faults of the literary historians I have cited, the most fundamental was that they franti-cally tried to establish inalterable continuities, refusing to envisage changes. It is not an accident that they must all be classed as conservatives.[10] Josef Nadler, who was their forerunner and probably the most articulate propo-nent of this thinking, keeps insisting on this point. He claims there was "a mystical unity between the poetic personality" and what he calls the "Staatsgemeinschaft" to which it belongs; he is convinced that whatever his-torical developments there were they had no impact on that national charac-ter ("die innere geistige Haltung des österreichischen Volkes haben sie nicht angetastet"); and he believes in an Austrian "Dichtung mit unwandelbaren Wesenszügen," a literature with immutable character traits.[11] This is politi-cal ideology, and immutability was one of its postulates for good reasons. Nadler's edifice collapses as soon as one no longer shares his axiomatic pre-suppositions.

Let me talk about continuities and discontinuities in my own way for a moment, using two larger categories: language and tradition. One of the fea-tures uniting many Austrians and at the same time distinguishing them from non-Austrians is their brand of German. (Naturally it is entirely conceivable for a Czech or Hungarian work to capture a peculiar moment or mood be-fore 1914, and thus be "Austrian" in the defined historical sense. That I am only considering authors writing in German is not meant to be ethnocentric. My selectivity merely takes cognizance of the fact that from our perspective the term "Austrian literature" implies the words "in the German lan-guage.") Indeed the linguistic tension between Austria and the other Ger-man-speaking areas is, as we shall see, a constitutive element of Austrian-ness. It is true, Austrian German is a branch of Bavarian. But it has its own history and its own idiosyncrasies. In vocabulary, syntax, tone, and social stratification, particularly through its Slavic and Italian admixtures, it reflects the multilingual and multicultural situation of the Danubian monar-chy. But even this Austrian German is not a uniform thing: the dialect of Salzburg is closer to that of Munich than to that of Vienna. The Tyrol has its own coarse tongue, in its remote forms hardly intelligible to Eastern Aus-trians. And the language of Vorarlberg, the westernmost province, is not Bavarian at all but Alemannic in character. This linguistic difference, inci-dentally, was advanced as the reason why Vorarlberg applied for member-ship in the Swiss Confederation right after the First World War, a time of economic hardship and feeble identity for Austria. The obvious question arising is this: Had Switzerland acceded to these wishes, and taken Vorarlberg to its bosom, would the literature written in and around Bregenz have become Swiss henceforth? Clearly, language is a unifying and dividing agent at one and the same time.

Even a brief survey suggests that works written in Vienna by Viennese authors are one thing and those produced in the provinces by provincial writers another, for linguistic as well as cultural reasons. Each branch may be "Austrian" in its own way, but as a rule they cannot be regarded as belonging together, making up an indivisible whole amenable to the same modes of explication. Of course, the vast majority of Viennese works is not written in dialect. Ordinarily they are written for the middle and upper middle classes by members of the same groups in a language that can be more or less close to the popular idiom, containing few or many recognizable Austriacisms, and possibly preserving some sort of Austrian tone. I am far from subscribing to the saw *Quod non est in lingua non est in mundo*, and am much more of the persuasion expressed in the Italian proverb *Fra il dire ed il fare c'è di mezzo il mare*. But I do believe that the dialect from which that language sprang, the cosmopolitan nature of the Hapsburg Empire, its court life, and other matters have left traces in it which enable us to detect the Austrian origin of at least some works. This is especially true when an author consciously exploits the Austrian flavor of the language—as did, for example, Karl Kraus and Herzmanovsky-Orlando, to mention only two. I am convinced that this linguistic difference would show up if a North German novelist were to write about a typically Austrian event, say the dissolution of the Monarchy and its causes. Musil's and Roth's accounts of the same phenomenon would probably have an additional Austrian tone.

The reason why so plausible a reflection should still strike us as so very tentative is the lack of scholarly investigation into this sphere. A fusion of historical and socio-linguistic methods would be called for here. There exist several descriptions of the Austrian dialects, but none that link them to their historical matrix, the peculiar structure of Austrian society under the Hapsburg rule.

Let me finally also point out that language, in spite of providing a strong continuity and identity, is anything but static itself. The vertical rise, for example, of the Viennese dialect into higher levels of society since World War II is one such dynamic change, and probably accounts for figures like Artmann and Qualtinger.

Several factors will have to be considered under the rubric of tradition. First of all, there are the objective givens of history. The Hapsburg dynasty, the multilingual aristocracies and armies of the Empire, a social structure that differed from other European societies, the role of Vienna as a centripetal force, the late advent of modernization must have left their imprints on the mentality of the people. The resulting impact of the more conservative forces—Catholicism, the Counterreformation, Spain, and the Baroque—on Austria, and the concomitant weaker impact of Protestantism and the Enlightenment, also help distinguish her culture from significant portions of Germany, particularly those under Prussian hegemony. Another factor is the presence of large masses of rural but mobile Jews in the Empire and their migration to Vienna from the late 18th century on.

Then there is the increasing distance of Austria from the other German-speaking territories. Whether one looks at the Seven Years' War, in which Austria was defeated by Prussia, and deprived of the rich province of Silesia; or the year 1806 when the Holy Roman Empire was officially dissolved; or the Bismarckian unification known as "kleindeutsch" and preceded by the Austrian defeat of 1866; or the prevention of a German-Austrian union after World War I, desired by many Austrians but prohibited by the victorious Allies; or the disastrous "Anschluß" effected under Hitler that did more for separation than all the alienating events before; or, finally, the different treatment of Austria by the occupational powers in 1955—there have been ample reasons for a socio-economic and cultural development of its own, the formation of a national ideology and a distinctive Austrian consciousness. The dynamic attraction and repulsion of the big neighbor to the Northwest from whom, in analogy to the British-American case, Austria is separated by the same language, constitutes itself a peculiar Austrian experience. From Grillparzer to Hofmannsthal, Musil, Broch, and beyond, this state of affairs has influenced Austrian literati profoundly.[12]

Because of this awareness, Austrian writers have often grown up under the influence of a different literary canon, in which Grillparzer loomed large as the founder of an Austrian consciousness. Needless to say, Grillparzer hardly enjoys the same high esteem in German schools, universities, theaters, and literary circles. As another consequence of this separate consciousness, many Austrian writers looked for models and contacts in France, England, and other countries before turning to Germany for inspiration. This fact notwithstanding, there is also their constant and almost morbid preoccupation with Germany, and the need to define themselves against the neighboring colossus.[13] Such a precarious identity is not aided by an often disturbing economic factor: It is much easier for a gifted Austrian writer to find a publisher in Germany than at home[14]

Here is what we can conclude from all these reminders and reservations. Because of certain historical circumstances Austria has led a separate life in some respects, but has also partaken of the destinies and developments of other portions of Europe, especially Germany. Due to the fragmentation of experience depending on place of birth, social, economic, and other conditions, it would be absurd to claim that all Austrian writers shared the same basic cultural and ideological concerns. It depends on the viewer's acumen, erudition, and intellectual orientation into what historical context he will place a work, an author, or a whole school. There can be no doubt that all literature that has originated in Austria, whether individual works or a whole body of them, stands in some nexus with Austrian history. To understand them this nexus will have to be studied and described. Thus one more question should be added to those already asked: *In what way* is a certain Austrian work of literature Austrian?

It seems to me that, in the case of Grillparzer, one would have to focus on his Josephinian heritage, his relation to Weimar classicism and other German phenomena, on his reactions to Austrian institutions of the time, to Spanish drama, and to the popular Viennese stage. All of these are very Austrian questions. Since Stifter was a contemporary of Grillparzer, one would have to consider similar things in his case, but also take into account the state of Catholic education, the situation of the church in general, the meaning of his flight into the provinces, and his reactions to the early stages of commercialization and industrialization in Austria. When dealing with the *fin de siècle* literature, one would need to examine the reasons for the extraordinary number of Jewish writers in Vienna, the role of antisemitism and liberalism, and the impact of these phenomena on the individual author. The dominant fact in the literature after 1918 was its fixation on the demise of the Austro-Hungarian Empire. To understand the various stances adopted toward this collapse by writers from Kraus to Roth and Musil, the literary scholar would himself have to become acquainted with the underlying historical realities.

Having reached this point in the chronology, the time is finally ripe for us to ask, by way of illustration, how H.C. Artmann and Helmut Qualtinger fit into the Viennese scene after World War II. Yet the moment one looks at Artmann and Qualtinger, a new uncertainty arises. Am I not shirking my responsibilities by choosing two authors who wrote in the Viennese dialect, or a language so close to and so colored by this dialect, that the very question of whether or not they are Austrian seems superfluous and even preposterous? But, as we have seen, language is only one of the criteria involved. If we focus on the social background, the affiliations are no longer so obvious. From this point of view, Artmann may seem farther removed from "Austrianness" than Qualtinger. The poems in his collection *med ana schwoazzn dintn*, which are responsible for his fame, have been described in terms of "surrealism" and "black humor," normally categories alien to dialect poetry. Artmann's "passion for comparative linguistics," his "extensive knowledge of foreign and remote literature," is routinely stressed. This sophistication and learnedness also remove him from the usual mold of folk poet. Another opinion frequently heard about Artmann's art stresses his unusual handling of the dialect itself. He "frees the dialect from its ghetto," enriches it with "inventions and neologisms," has made it a vehicle "for modern poetry," *etc*. These statements culminate in the surprised question:

"Warum waren uns Mundartgedichte eigentlich so unerträglich?"[15] It is apparent that Artmann, the avant-gardist, destroyed the customary expectations and forced his readers to change their minds about the medium he was using. These expectations are easy enough to reconstruct. Ever since Goethe's famous remarks, dialect was supposed to be close to "the people," to "the emotions," "the soil," "the autochthonous." The "Beschränkung auf eine bestimmte Mundart [schien] automatisch eine geistige Beschränkung und eine . . . der Themenwahl zu bedingen"; the writer felt he had to adopt "eine simple Mentalität" together with the dialect, and therefore dialect poems appeared "durch ihren gewollt biederen Tonfall albern und durch die Wiederholung derselben Motive eintönig."[16] Artmann liberated the dialect from this ballast. Without casting away the emotional advantages inherent in the language of the people, he rose to unexpected intellectual and artistic heights.

Another Austrian poet from the proletarian suburbs, Ernst Waldinger, had celebrated, as a refugee in New York, the traditional values of the dialect in a poem which itself was not free from the sentimentality attributed to its subject:

Wienerisch

Leicht nasal und weich wie ein Kalfakter
Unter allen deutschen Dialekten,
Süffig, doch gefährlich, gleich den Sekten
Unter Weinen, ohne den Charakter
Preußisch schnarrender Kommandotöne,
Sehr melodisch, offen für das Schöne

Ist mein Wienerisch aus Ottakring,
Das ich in der Kinderzeit empfangen,
Lieder, die aus Leierkästen klangen,
Die ich heute noch im Traume sing,
Meine Sprache tanzend und verschwebend,
Anmutreich auf meinen Lippen lebend,

Noch das Englische in jedem Laute,
Das im neuen Land ich rede, färbend,
Sanftheit jenes Alten ihm vererbend
Und der Schwermut leise, innig-traute
Stimme, jedes fremde Wort beseelend,
Meine Abkunft niemals ganz verhehlend.[17]

The dimension alluded to by the single word "gefährlich," whatever Waldinger might have had in mind, is brought forth vigorously by Artmann. As a matter of fact, his introductory poem, which one may regard as programmatic, rejects the maudlin mode of dialect poetry in the very first line:

> nua ka schmoez how e xogt!
> nua ka schmoez ned . . .

It continues in an even more explicit, albeit ironic tone:

> reis s ausse dei heazz dei bluadex
> und hau s owe iwa r a bruknglanda!

The last stanza finally pronounces with unsurpassable resoluteness the break with the warmth and primitivity of the usual kind of dialect poems. In its reference to the city borough of Ottakring, the stanza seems to be a direct reply to Waldinger:

> Waun owa r ana r a gedicht schreim wüü
> und iwahaupt no a weaneresch dazua
> daun sol a zeascht med sei heazz
> med sein bozwachn . . .
> nur recht schnöö noch otagring ausse
> oda sunztwo zu an bruknglanda gee![18]

Instead, Artmann emphasizes the cruelty, the sadism, the demonism, the cynical brutality, and a dozen other propensities of the lower class district which history has recorded, but which the legend refuses to acknowledge. Such poems as the one about the "ringlschbüübsizza" ("blauboad"), a fear-ridden sex maniac who kills his wives and girlfriends; the uncanny nursery rhyme "kindafazara," with the infantile refrain "kölaschdiang köla-schdiang"; or the "liad fon an besn geatna," with its nihilistic "Schadenfreude," and many others combine perverted humor, dread, and latent violence,[19] expressing to perfection the neurotic streak and barely controlled resentment that slumbers beneath the proverbial "golden heart" of the Viennese lower middle classes. In this sense, it may be argued, the poems reveal their origin in the post-second-world-war period. Another oblique connection between Artmann and his public of the 1950's may be sought, even if it won't be easy to prove, in the changed sociological function of the dialect. Be it because of the departure of the educated and art-loving Jewish population, or because of a deliberate assertion of the dialect against the Nazi presence in Austria as an act of resistance, or because of the greater economic affluence of the lower middle classes: the dialect, during the war and postwar years, rose into social strata where it hadn't been before. If one assumes that, consciously or unconsciously, Artmann had this more sophisticated dialect public in mind when he wrote *med ana schwoazzn dintn*—and reception theory encourages one to make this assumption—then it is possible to interpret the coming into existence of these poems as another indirect result of the changed cultural situation after 1945.

But if one looks for direct references to the historical moment, the yield is minimal. And therefore, in spite of the language and the innumerable local realia in them, one is tempted to agree with Artmann's friend and interpreter Friedrich Polakovics who wrote in his introduction: "Artmanns Dialektgedichte sind keine *Dialekt*gedichte. Auch keine Wiener Gedichte, sondern Gedichte aus Wien."[20]

The opposite is certainly true of Helmut Qualtinger, who is a cabaretist through and through and as such a social critic. Everything he has done is satirical in nature and bears direct reference to the social and political realities of the day or decade. Whether his target is political corruption or bureaucratic favoritism, collusion between press and police to the detriment of criminal detection and law enforcement, the traffic chaos in Vienna and the ineptitude of the regulatory agencies, Austria's unresolved relationship to the fascist past, both the German and the local brand—the satirist trains his powerful gaze on the foibles and anomalies in his social environment. The underlying conviction is that of the psychoanalyst and enlightenment rationalist, both of whom believe in the cure of social and mental disorders by bringing them into the light of consciousness. But since the psycho-historian deals with ingrained patterns of feeling and behavior, a curious *double entendre* obtains here: The closer Qualtinger sticks to the here and now, the more his reader experiences a *déjà vu*. Often one has the irresistible feeling that one is dealing with the First Republic, indeed the Danubian monarchy. Instinctively, Qualtinger seems to agree. With his television play, "Alles gerettet,"[21] he, too, turns to the past for the purpose of illuminating the present. Here he shows his true colors unadulterated. Like most satirists, he is a moral philosopher as well. By reconstructing the trial following the famous Ringtheater fire of 1882, in which hundreds of persons perished, he can raise the question of individual and collective responsibility, so to speak, *in abstracto*. The historical setting permits him to sever the entanglements between his audiences and the subject matter that prevent them from recognizing their complicity with contemporary malfeasances. The result is a denouncement of the outrageous Viennese inability to determine guilt. We have before us a superb example for the persistence of the old in the new. *Plus ça change . . .*

The creation of Travnicek,[22] the predecessor of Herr Karl, enabled Qualtinger to embody the disparate elements of a socio-psychological ailment in a single personage, a composite but believable type. With the aid of clever dialog, plays on words, and other humoristic devices, the essentially antisocial, prejudice-ridden personality of the Viennese petit-bourgeois emerges, and an unmasking of protagonist and environment through one another is enacted on a grand scale.

But the undisputed masterpiece of this kind of fictitious self-denouncement of the lower middle-class mentality is *Der Herr Karl*. This creation represents a high point of postwar literature, the culmination of the Austrian version of *Vergangenheitsbewältigung*. Qualtinger's literary cleansing act must, and wondrously can, stand for the many Nazi trials that ought to have taken place in Austria, but didn't. No extraordinary powers of clairvoyance are required to recognize in this frightening monolog the portrait of vast masses of Austrians. There is ample testimony that even those segments of the population whom the figure of Herr Karl pillories understood the indictment. The meaning of the thousands of indignant responses, epistolary or by telephone, to the public performance of *Der Herr Karl* can be summarized in one word: *Touché.*[23] The secret of its success lies in the combination of an obvious socio-psychological pathology with the inexorable historicity of the background. Thus, there obtains a dynamic paradox: Precisely through the localization of both character and events, their significance is vastly expanded beyond its sharply defined boundaries. Karl, whose social class is the petite bourgeoisie, whose operating radius is restricted to the municipal area of Vienna (one of his reminiscences reveals an almost total incapacity for relating to the Austria beyond the capital), and whose time range encompasses no more than the two Republics with the war in between, has become an all-Austrian character, an heir to Karl Kraus's "Österreichisches Antlitz," indeed the highly politicized image of the apolitical, abysmally vacuous European fellow traveler. Moral obtuseness, exploitation of others, especially women, treachery, inability to work, sexual voyeurism, incipient pyromania, aestheticistic anti-humanism, political prostitution, unprincipled opportunism of every sort: these are the terrifying counts of the verdict, an X-ray picture of modern mass man.

If our analysis of Artmann's *med ana schwoazzn dintn* established at the most a circuitous, largely atmospheric connection between the poetic word and the historical fact, in *Der Herr Karl* we encounter an almost complete synonymity of the two. Artmann's dialect poems possess an artistic quality that transcends, as do Qualtinger's best satires, the local and the temporal. In most of his other publications, Artmann is even farther removed from the post-war Austrian scene. But in one work at least he returns to it, establishing a rapport with the Vienna of the 1950's and 1960's that rivals Qualtinger's proximity to the period. I am referring to Artmann's stories *Von der Wiener Seite.*[24] On the surface, these short pieces of prose, suffused with dialect, seem innocuous, even pointless vignettes of Viennese folk life. Closer inspection reveals, however, that the majority of them portray encounters between the happy-go-lucky, *gemütlich* Viennese mentality and the creeping infiltration of something new, often mechanized. In one of the episodes, "Die Oase in der Opernpassage,"[25] we are shown the not entirely happy *liaisons* between the postwar type of *süßes Mädel*, somewhat seedier than Schnitzler's prototypes, and the ubiquitous Arab foreigners. In another, entitled "Herr Morawetz motorisiert sich,"[26] the reader witnesses the ill-fated acquisition of a moped by a middle-aged Viennese married couple. A third, "Herr Adamek schreibt einen Bestseller,"[27] satirizes the allurements and absurd consequences of publishing in the technically more advanced markets of Germany. In another yet, significantly named "Keine Menschenfresser, bitte!",[28] two ancient Viennese evils, xenophobia and landlady greed, are mocked by the arrival of the prospective roomer who turns out to be the desired American, but at the same time disappoints expectations by being black. Lighthearted and conciliatory as their treatment may be, each of these episodes depicts the confrontation between a psychological continuity and an instance of disruptive change. It will be remembered that we have defined social history precisely in these terms!

Perhaps the most tell-tale of these sketches is one where Artmann, in the first person and undisguisedly speaking of himself, describes the collision of the old and the new in the Café Hawelka, a kind of Griensteidl of the 1950's.[29] In spite of the brevity of the piece, Artmann's difficulty in deciding for the Old or the New Vienna causes his reflections to follow a meandering line. At first the "Hawelka" is termed with obvious approval "das schönste Stadtcafé von altem Schrot und Korn": the owner shakes hands with the habitués, the chief waiter lords it over the customers, one can get one's "Nußbeugeln und Melangen" (the title of the sketch) as well as the traditional "Ei im Glas." The writers and artists continue to live their unharried coffeehouse existence. Without the "Hawelka," a great deal would remain "ungetan, ungesprochen oder von Grund aus gar nicht mehr erdacht"—in other words, it still is a typically Viennese cultural center "für uns wie für unsere Vorfahren." Thus six decades have been absorbed "ohne die geringste Spur."

But then an Espresso machine was installed, symbol of our technological "gehetzte, mond- und raketennarrische Zeit." In the beginning, Mr. Hawelka tendered the excuse that the innovation was needed to defray the "Gasgeld," and everybody agreed with this euphemism. Soon, however, the deeper underlying motives came to the fore: people want progress, modernity. "Mia san jo net hintan Mond!" Eventually, even the most inveterate *laudatores temporis acti* admitted that they had been dissatisfied with the old conditions, that they had become incurably tired of the "ungelüfteter Plüsch der Vergangenheit," the loose steel springs of the seats, "die immer im ungeeigneten Moment eine gewisse Stelle unserer Beinkleider durchbohrten." In short, they seemed to have outgrown the coffeehouse, symbol of Old Vienna, and greeted the advent of the first *Espressi all'italiana* as harbingers of progress, "wie die Morgenröte einer schöneren, besseren Welt." Thus a typical pattern of Austrian history appears to have repeated itself: after long resistance to innovation, the inevitable change sets in and is accepted by the population.

But this is not the final conclusion. Artmann ends with an unexpected twist. The vitality of the old Viennese coffeehouse had been underestimated, which is to say that Viennese conservatism cannot be overcome so easily. Espresso machines, it is true, were triumphant all over the place, but a regressive tendency is secretly at work and, in the last analysis, snatches away victory:

> Fast alle Espressi, von der inneren Stadt heraus bis in die Peripherie, was sind sie denn als etwas modernisierte "Cafés" und urgemütliche Tschocherln, in denen man bei einem kleinen Braunen stundenlang plaudert, tarockiert oder preferanct, den Ober oder die Serviererin höflich mit Herr Josef oder Fräulein Rita tituliert, in denen man sich genau so benimmt und genau so genommen wird, wie seinerzeit im guten alten Café.

It does not matter much that in his allegory Artmann allows the psychological continuity of Viennese tradition to triumph over newfangled mechanization. The important point is not the outcome, which is the result of subjective preferences, but the perception of the ongoing battle, which is the expression of objective supra-individual forces, and that this struggle is couched, sketch after sketch, in the unmistakable terms of postwar Viennese reality.

It is not difficult to draw a few lessons even from such a cursory discussion of our two authors. Despite their opposing stances as a *l'art pour l'art* and an *engagé* writer, respectively, they have more in common than meets the eye trained only in textual analysis, or blinded by preconceived notions. This common ground is provided by the Viennese social milieu. We can sum up our experiences with Artmann and Qualtinger by tentatively answering the questions raised in the beginning. Yes, there is an Austrian literature because there is an Austrian historical reality. Every work of literature emerging from this reality reflects it in some way and is bound to be impregnated with elements of the Austrian experience. Only by carefully matching the two spheres, the literary and the socio-historical, not through the clichés of cultural autonomy or an outmoded ethnic irrationalism, can one get a glimpse of their intricate relationship. The advantages of doing so are obvious: Without giving up the benefits of documentation and scholarly verisimilitude, one can determine the features tying together individual authors, disparate works, and literary schools, and construct a mosaic out of what would otherwise remain isolated and unrelated fragments. Thus a semblance of the long lost unity of culture can be recaptured.

But "Austria" is not a concept of overpowering density or all-pervasive centrality. Its history was not a steady embroidery of the same continuous strands. Many forces invaded the tenuous boundaries of what can be described as Austrian, and shaped its destinies. The same reservation holds true for any nation in the world, but it is particularly valid in connection with this elusive culture. Therefore one will have to focus on relatively small units of time, space, and society in order to determine the mode of interaction between literary works and the epochs in which they originated. Because of the freedom, no matter how circumscribed, which every individual retains, and because of the infinite variety of influences shaping an author, this method will expose the peculiar reciprocities between him and his environment—in other words, his very own way of being Austrian. Brief as the analysis of our two authors has been, it is sufficient to show that each belongs undeniably to the Viennese scene after 1945, but also responded in his own individual manner to their common challenges.

A literary work is caught in a complex net of relationships, and there are many contexts in which it functions. I am very far from claiming the method I have sketchily delineated to be the only legitimate one for dealing with an Austrian work. But if we want to focus on its *Austrianness*, mine strikes me as a plausible approach.

[1]Compare my two articles in which I have argued similarly: "Joseph Roth und die österreichische Literatur," in *Joseph Roth und die Tradition* (Darmstadt: Agora Verlag, 1975); "Die sechste Schwierigkeit beim Schreiben der Wahrheit: Zum Gruppendenken in Leben und Literatur," in *Die USA und Deutschland: Wechselseitige Spiegelungen in der Literatur der Gegenwart*, hrsg. von Wolfgang Paulsen (Bern: Francke Verlag, 1976).

[2]See fn. 7 below.

[3]*Das große Erbe: Aufsätze zur österreichischen Literatur* von Otto Basil, Herbert Eisenreich, Ivar Ivask (Graz/Wien: Stiasny Verlag, 1962).

[5]Ibid., pp. 106ff.

[5]Ibid., pp. 40f.

[6]Ibid., pp. 88f.

[7]Gerhart Baumann, "Österreich als Dichtung," in *Spectrum Austriae,* hrsg. von Otto Schulmeister (Wien: Verlag Herder, 1957).

[8]Ibid., pp. 583ff.

[9]Hans Weigel, *Flucht vor der Größe: Beiträge zur Erkenntnis und Selbsterkenntnis Österreichs* (Wien: Wollzeilen Verlag, 1960). All following quotations are from pp. 9-12 of this work.

[10]Literary critics and historians are not the only ones to blame. One must only think of Hugo von Hofmannsthal's much-quoted comparison "Preuße-Österreicher" and such personifications of North Germany as Baron Neuhoff in his comedy *Der Schwierige* to realize that the poets have indulged in the same pastime. One could chalk this off as the whim of a traditionalist Austrian and conservative in the "kleindeutsch" manner, which Hofmannsthal after all was, if the figures of such repulsive Prussians did not occur in other Austrian works as well. What happens is that some writers attributed the collapse of the traditional order, in which they were radicated, to the threat of something new they identified vaguely but not incorrectly with modernism, technology, and industrialization. But they mistakenly accused the Prussians of having caused such phenomena, making them into incarnations of these destructive forces. The aristocratic Prussian society in turn, threatened by the same economic developments, had to find, again assisted by its literature, other scapegoats such as the Jews, the English, or the Americans. We have here a superb example of the political potential inherent in "national characterology."

[11]Josef Nadler, "Die deutsche Dichtung Österreichs," in *Österreich: Erbe und Sendung im deutschen Raum*, hrsg. von Josef Nadler und Heinrich von Srbik (Salzburg/Leipzig: Anton Pustet Verlag, 1936), pp. 324f.

[12]I should like to round out these reflections by reconstructing from my own memory how a schoolboy experienced the Austrian scene between the two wars and how some of the factors just mentioned became united in his biography. As a Viennese, I grew up in the unshakable conviction that there was something German about Austria, but that Austrian and German were anything but synonymous terms. To put it bluntly: In my circles, Germany was re-

garded as enemy territory, and it was very disquieting to know that many Austrians held the opposite view. A great number of the threats and disruptions of which I was aware as a child and adolescent emanated from this powerful neighbor whose habit it was to come on strong, either as an individual tourist or as an agent of international politics. And indeed, as is common knowledge, it was that power which, on March 11, 1939, put an end to Austrian independence.

Our feeling that Austrianness was something quite distinctive, worth understanding and preserving, encompassed literature as well. In the Gymnasium, it is true, we read Goethe, Schiller, Rosegger, Raimund, Nestroy, Gerstäcker, Storm, Stifter, and Mell quite indiscriminately, but from the works of the Austrian writers there seemed to flow a different breeze, be it because of local allusions to landmarks in Vienna and the surrounding landscape, or because of certain peculiarities of language.

We were reinforced in our cultural and political stance in favor of Austrian independence by the arrival of the first refugees from the recently installed Hitler regime in Germany, who found their way into our Gymnasium. Teachers and students alike were thrown into tizzies of amazement at the language of these unfortunate newcomers. Their speech resembled our customary German in some respects, but was miles apart from it in its total effect. I remember that our Latin professor caused paroxysms of laughter by making the new North Germans read certain passages again and again. The roar caused by the single word "Romanorumque," with its uvular "r's" and the muffled "u," must have been audible as far as the outskirts of Vienna.

When Austro-Fascism made its appearance, even those of us who were opposed to the regime realized it was the last barrier between us and a Hitler takeover. When Dollfuß was murdered by Austrian Nazis, and we were forced to sing the insipid hymn,

> Ihr Jungen schließt die Reihen gut,
> Ein Toter führt euch an,
> Er gab für Österreich sein Blut,
> Ein wahrer deutscher Mann,

we sensed that, in all its absurdity, there was something utterly realistic in its twisted expression of hostile identity between what was German and what was Austrian.

And well after the collapse, as a refugee in various European countries and later in South America, when I met German-speaking fugitives from all parts of the dialect map, my Austrian consciousness asserted itself again. In spite of the common fate, the linguistic, cultural, and even psychological differences persisted. As I grew older and expanded my intellectual horizon, these issues drifted into the background, but I suspect that childhood experiences are too strong to disappear entirely. Somehow they must still be elements of my personality.

[13]There are several excellent scholarly works that deal with segments of the interrelationship between Austrian literature and social history. I shall cite a few. Notably, there are the highly suggestive essays by Carl E. Schorske, in *Fin-de-siècle Vienna: Politics and Culture* (New York: Knopf, 1980), as well as Allan Janik and Stephen Toulmin, *Wittgenstein's Vienna* (New York: Simon and Schuster, 1973). Other works include: C.E. Williams, *The Broken Eagle: The Politics of Austrian Literature from Empire to Anschluß* (New York: Harper & Row, 1974); Claudio Magris, *Il mito absburgico nella letteratura austriaca moderna* (Torino, 1963); Wolfram Mauser, *Hugo von Hofmannsthal: Konfliktbewältigung und Werkstruktur. Eine psychosoziologische Interpretation* (München: Wilhelm Fink Verlag, 1977); Rolf-Peter Janz / Klaus Laermann, *Arthur Schnitzler: Zur Diagnose des Wiener Bürgertums im Fin de siècle* (Stuttgart: Metzlersche Verlagsbuchhandlung, 1977).

[14]This also goes for the reading public. It has been said that Viennese writers are "vom inländischen Publikum mehr als andernorts ignoriert"; cf. Peter O. Chotjewitz, "Der neue selbstkolorierte Dichter," in *Über H.C. Artmann,* hrsg. von Gerald Bisinger (Frankfurt: Suhrkamp Verlag, 1972), p. 13.

[15]Wieland Schmied, "Der Dichter H.C. Artmann," ibid., pp. 42f.

[16]Ibid.

[17]Quoted by Mimi Grossberg, "Der New Yorker literarische Kreis von 1938," *Literatur und Kritik*, No. 119 (Oktober 1977), p. 551.

[18]H.C. Artmann, *med ana schwoazzn dintn: gedichta r aus bradnsee* (Salzburg: Otto

Müller Verlag, 1958), p. 7.

[19]See pp. 17f., 19, and 20. There are, of course, also tender childhood and love poems in this collection.

[20]Ibid., p. 16.

[21]*Qualtingers beste Satiren: Vom Travnicek zum Herrn Karl*, mit Texten von Helmut Qualtinger, Gerhard Bronner und Carl Merz, hrsg. von Brigitte Erbacher (Wien: Langen Müller Verlag, 1973), pp. 225ff.

[22]Ibid., pp. 95ff.

[23]A composite version of such letters is published in the above *Satiren*, pp. 316ff., with the insightful closing: "Ergebenst Ihr Herr Karl" (Wien I, II, III, IV, V, VI, VII, VIII, IX, X, XI, XII, XIII, XIV, XV, XVI, XVII, XVIII, XIX, XX, XXI, XXII; also Graz, Linz, Salzburg, Innsbruck, *etc.*).

[24]H.C. Artmann, *Von der Wiener Seite: Geschichten* (Berlin: Literarisches Colloquium, 1972).

[25]Ibid., pp. 14ff.

[26]Ibid., pp. 67ff.

[27]Ibid., pp. 70ff.

[28]Ibid., pp. 61ff.

[29]Ibid., pp. 11ff.

Library of Congress Cataloging in Publication Data
Main entry under title:
From Kafka and Dada to Brecht and beyond.
(Monatshefte occasional volume; no. 2)
Revised lectures originally presented at
Oberlin College, 1976–1981.
Includes bibliographical references.
Contents: Kafka's poetics of the inner self /
Walter H. Sokel—Varieties of phonetic poetry /
Peter Demetz—Confessions of a poet /
Reinhold Grimm—[etc.]
1. German literature—20th century—History and
criticism—Addresses, essays, lectures.   2. German
literature—Austrian authors—History and criticism
—Addresses, essays, lectures.   I. Demetz, Peter,
1922–   . II. Grimm, Reinhold.   III. Spycher,
Peter C., 1921–   .   IV. Zipser, Richard A.
V. Series.
PT403.F73   830′.9′0091   81–24056
ISBN 0–299–97014–0   AACR2